Microsoft Dynamics CRM 2011 Online
Quick Reference

ALSO BY THE AUTHORS

Maximizing Your Sales with Microsoft Dynamics CRM 2011

Microsoft Dynamics CRM Online 2011 Tips & Tricks

Maximizing Your Sales with Salesforce.com

90 Days to Success in Fundraising

90 Days to Success in Grant Writing

Managing Contacts with Outlook Business Contact Manager

Managing Contacts with ACT!

Microsoft Dynamics CRM 2011 Online

Quick Reference

Edward Kachinske

Timothy Kachinske

Adam Kachinske

Innovative Solutions | *Washington, DC*

Published in the United States and United Kingdom by Innovative Solutions in Washington, DC.
www.is-crm.com

Cataloging-in-Publication Data is on file with the Library of Congress.

Kachinske, Edward; Kachinske, Timothy; Kachinske, Adam
Microsoft Dynamics CRM Online 2011 Quick Reference (Paperback) 2nd Edition

ISBN: 0-9706069-9-0
ISBN 13: 978-0-9706069-9-0

PRINTED IN THE UNITED STATES OF AMERICA

10 9 8 7 6 5 4 3 2 1

About the Authors

Edward Kachinske has written more than 25 books on CRM-related topics, including Maximizing Your Sales with Microsoft Dynamics CRM, Maximizing Your Sales with Salesforce.com, Managing Contacts with Outlook, the Official ACT! Course Manuals for Instructor-Led Training, and more. He is a frequent speaker at CRM-related conferences and is on the Microsoft Dynamics EC Advisory Board.

Edward is the President of Innovative Solutions, a Gold Certified Microsoft Dynamics CRM Partner. Innovative Solutions is a Microsoft Dynamics President's Club member, ranking in the top 5% for sales of Microsoft Dynamics CRM worldwide. Edward is certified in Microsoft Dynamics CRM and is a Microsoft Certified Trainer. He holds a dozen other Microsoft certifications, including the Microsoft Certified IT Professional status.

Timothy Kachinske has written more than a dozen books on CRM and non-profit management topics. Titles written by Tim include Maximizing Your Sales with Microsoft Dynamics CRM, Maximizing Your Sales with Salesforce.com, 90 Days to Success in Fundraising, and 90 Days to Success in Grant Writing. He has 17 years of experience as a development officer for various non-profit organizations, and has been designing CRM solutions for NFP organizations for more than a decade.

Tim teaches an online class on Microsoft Dynamics CRM and a class on non-profit fundraising through a consortium of colleges and universities. Through this consortium, Tim's classes are distributed to more than 1,500 colleges and universities in North America. Tim is a Microsoft Certified Trainer and is certified in Microsoft Dynamics CRM and SharePoint.

Adam Kachinske is a CRM consultant for Innovative Solutions in Washington, DC. In addition to this book, Adam is an author of Maximizing Your Sales with Microsoft Dynamics CRM 2011 and the Innovative Solutions set of Microsoft Dynamics CRM Quick Reference Cards. He is a Microsoft Certified Technical Specialist for Microsoft Dynamics CRM and SharePoint.

Table of Contents

1

Setting up CRM Online

Signing up for a CRM Online Trial

You'd probably be disappointed if you bought Microsoft Dynamics CRM Online only to find out that you didn't like it. This is why Microsoft offers you a free thirty day trial of Dynamics CRM Online.

This trial will give you the chance to use Microsoft Dynamics CRM and decide whether or not you want to buy it. You can activate into a paid subscription at any time over the course of the trial period. If you don't activate you will lose your data.

Step-by-Step Instructions

1. In Internet Explorer (not Firefox) go to http://crm.dynamics.com.

2. Click on the **Get Started** button under the Free Trial header.

3. Select your country and click Submit.

4. Enter the required information to activate your trial.

Tips & Tricks

➢ Trials last for thirty days.

➢ At the end of thirty days, you can sign up for another trial, but none of your data would come over into the new trial database.

https://signup.**live.com**/signup.aspx?lic=1

View   Favorites   Tools   Help

Suggested Sites • Web Slice Gallery

Windows Live

indows Live™

Create your Windows Live ID

It gets you into all Windows Live services—and other places you see
All information is required.

If you use **Hotmail**, **Messenger**, or **Xbox LIVE**, you already have a Windows Live ID. Sign in

Use your email address: *Example: someone@example.com*

Or get a Windows Live email address

Create a password:

8-character minimum; case sensitive

Retype password:

First name:

Last name:

Obtaining a Windows Live ID

You'll need a Windows live ID before you can do anything in Microsoft Dynamics CRM Online. Fortunately, you don't have to pay a dime for a Windows Live ID, and it can be used to log into other Microsoft websites – like Bing, Zune, Xbox, etc.

Step-by-Step Instructions

1. Type https://signup.live.com in the address bar of Internet Explorer. (Don't forget the "s" in https.)

2. Enter in the required information.

3. Click **I Accept.**

Tips & Tricks

➢ If you have a Hotmail account, you can link your Hotmail account to another Windows Live ID. Once you sign up for a Windows Live ID using your business e-mail address, you'll have an option to link the accounts. Then, if you're logged into your business Windows Live ID, you won't have to log out to check your personal Hotmail e-mail.

➢ If you have many users running Microsoft Dynamics CRM Online, you should ask your consultant or Microsoft rep about options for creating multiple Windows Live IDs. By default, you can only create 2 per IP address per day.

Logging into CRM Online

Microsoft Dynamics CRM Online is a web-based application, which means that you don't need to install any software on your computer. No more CDs, no more lost serial keys, and no more installing software! Instead, the application runs in Microsoft Internet Explorer or as a lightweight plugin in Outlook.

Microsoft Dynamics CRM Online will only work on a computer running Microsoft Windows XP SP2 or better. Microsoft Internet Explorer 6.0 SP2 or higher is also required. And if you're still using Outlook 2002 or older, climb out from under your rock, install Outlook 2003+, and try again.

Step-by-Step Instructions

1. Go directly to **yourname**.crm.dynamics.com. Substitute **yourname** for your organization's database name. Ask your administrator if you unsure of the URL name.

2. Enter your Windows Live ID and password. Click **Sign In**.

Tips & Tricks

➢ Choose Remember Password if you don't want to type your password every time you log in.

➢ Go to this web site to reset your Windows Live ID if you've forgotten your e-mail address: account.live.com/ResetPassword.aspx

sign in

Windows Live ID:

| |

Password:

| |

Forgot your password?

☑ Remember me
☐ Remember my password

[Sign in]

Activating your trial to a paid subscription

You can't get away with using the free trial of Microsoft Dynamics CRM forever, so at some point during the thirty days you will want to activate to a paid subscription.

Don't worry about any of the data in your trial subscription – it will still be in the same spot once you activate the paid subscription. If you don't activate, all of your data will be lost 30 days after the subscription expires.

Step-by-Step Instructions

1. Click **Settings** in the Navigation Pane then **System**, and then click **Administration**.

2. Click **Subscription Management** and then choose the option to convert your subscription to a paid offer.

3. Enter the required information to activate your account. (Have your credit card handy.)

Tips & Tricks

➤ Only the person who originally signed up for the trial will be able to activate.

➤ Call 877-CRM-CHOICE, option 2 if you need help activating.

2

Using Records

Creating a new record

You can't have a database without data, so you will need to learn how to create records before using Microsoft Dynamics CRM.

Accounts, contacts, leads, opportunities, and activities are all examples of records. They are the meat and potatoes of your database, and creating them is simple.

Step-by-Step Instructions

1. Click **Sales** in the **Navigation Pane**, and then click **Contacts**.

2. Click the **New** button in the Records group of the ribbon.

3. Enter information about the record. Click **Save and Close**.

Tips & Tricks

➤ Instead of creating records from scratch, you can import from an existing data source, like an Excel spreadsheet. Just click the Import Data button in the Data group of the ribbon.

Deleting or deactivating a record

Have you ever gotten into an argument with one of your contacts and thought, "Wow, I'd like to wipe you from my database?" Microsoft Dynamics CRM allows you to do this by either deleting or deactivating a record.

Deleted records can't be retrieved, so be careful before you delete a record. A deactivated record stays in the database with an inactive status, but won't appear in your active records.

Step-by-Step Instructions

1. Click **Sales** in the **Navigation Pane**, and then click **Contacts**.

2. Highlight the contact that you want to delete.

3. In the Records group of the ribbon, click the **Delete** icon. (It looks like an X.)

4. Click **Yes** to confirm the deletion.

Tips & Tricks

➢ This process walks you through the steps required to delete a contact, but these steps will work on just about any entity in the system.

➢ If you don't see an option to delete, you might not have access to delete records.

Importing records

Entering in records manually is a hassle. If your data already exists in electronic format, you'll need to learn to import records.

You might, for instance, have a spreadsheet of records that you want in CRM. By importing this file, you can spend less time entering data and more time selling or playing Solitaire.

Step-by-Step Instructions

1. Click **Sales** in the **Navigation Pane**, and then click **Contacts**. (To import records of a different type, do this process from another entity).

2. Click the **Import Data** button in the Data group of the ribbon.

3. Click **Browse** and look for your file. Click Next.

4. Select the type of record and data map. Click **Next**

5. Select a record owner and click **Next**.

6. Give the import a name and click **Import**.

Tips & Tricks

➢ You can import XML, CSV, TXT, and other basic data files into CRM. If your data is currently in another format, like ACT! or Goldmine, then you may consider having a consultant run your import to maintain notes, histories, activities, opportunities, etc.

Defining connections

Relationships can be hard to manage. Fortunately, Microsoft Dynamics CRM can help you keep track of a complicated relationship between different types of records in your database.

In Microsoft Dynamics CRM you can define connections, which can then be applied to records in your database.

Step-by-Step Instructions

1. Open an account or contact record.

2. On the left, click the **Connections** option. All of the existing connections for this record will appear.

3. Click the **Connect** button on the ribbon to create a new connection between this record and almost any other record in your system.

Tips & Tricks

➤ Before setting a connection, you should have roles set up in the system. Go to Settings | Business Management | Connection Roles. This is covered on the next page.

➤ You can link a record to yourself or another user using Connections.

➤ Any type of record can be connected, not just contacts or accounts. You can even connect a record to a user in your system.

Creating connections roles

Connection Roles

Create, edit, and delete the standard labels used to define connections between records.

Before you start connecting records in your database, you will need to create different connection roles. Once you've created a connection role, you can then apply this role any time you connect two records in your database.

Step-by-Step Instructions

1. Click **Settings** in the **Navigation Pane,** then **Business**, and then **Business Management**.

2. Click **Connection Roles**.

3. Click the **New** button on the toolbar.

4. Configure your connection role and click **Save & Close**.

Tips & Tricks

➢ CRM comes with built in default connection roles. Before you create a role, make sure that it is not already in your system.

Assigning records to other users or teams

Assign Contact
You have selected 1 Contact. To whom would you like to assign it?

⦿ **Assign to me**
Assign the selected Contact to yourself.

○ **Assign to another user or team**
Assign the selected Contact to the following user or team:

[　　　　　　　　　　　　　　　　　　　　] 🔍

| Help | | OK | Cancel |

Look Up Record
Enter your search criteria and click Search to find matching records. Filter your results and view different columns of data by using the View options. Then, select the record you want and click OK.

Look for: [User ▾]

View: [User Lookup View ▾]

Search: [Search for records 🔍]

| | Full Name ▲ | Main Phone | 🗘 |
| □ 👤 | Edward Kachinske | | CF |

1 - 1 of 1 (0 selected) |◄ ◄ Page 1 ►

[Properties] [New]

[OK] [Cancel] [Remove Value]

Do you have an annoying customer that you want to unload onto the guy in the cubicle next to yours? Fortunately, Microsoft Dynamics CRM lets you re-assign records to other users.

Whenever you create a new record, you are the owner of that record. You can re-assign ownership of the record as long as you have the user rights to do so.

Step-by-Step Instructions

1. Click **Sales**, then **Accounts** on the **Navigation Pane**.

2. Highlight the record you want assign.

3. Click the **Assign** button in the Collaborate group of the ribbon. (It looks like a person with an arrow.)

4. Choose a user to whom you'd like to assign the record, or assign it to yourself.

Tips & Tricks

➢ You may not have access to assign records in your system, so if you get an error, contact your system administrator.

Sharing records with other users or teams

Sharing is an important virtue – one that we all learned when we were young. Well, sharing is also a feature built into Microsoft Dynamics CRM.

Your database might be set up so that only a record owner can see his or her own records. A record owner then has the option to share his or her record with another user or team.

Step-by-Step Instructions

1. Click **Sales**, then **Accounts** on the **Navigation Pane**.

2. Highlight the account you want to share.

3. Click the **Share** button in the Collaborate group of the ribbon.

4. Click **Add User/Team** and find the user or team you'd like to share the record with.

Tips & Tricks

➤ These steps are written for accounts, but you can share any record in the system by clicking the Share button in the Collaborate group of the ribbon.

| File | Message | Insert | Options | Format Text | Rev |

Paste | Show | Basic Text | Names | Include | Track | Set Regarding
Clipboard

To...
Cc...
Subject: Adrian Dumitrascu (sample)

Adrian Dumitrascu (sample)
<https://crmquickreferencebook.crm.dynamics.com/ma
bf69-1cc1def127f4&pagetype=entityrecord>

Copying / sending shortcuts to records

So the guy in the cube next to you didn't go to CRM training. And he asked you *again* to look up someone's phone number.

Instead of just giving him the number, you could give him a shortcut to the record in CRM, and as long as he's a valid CRM user, he could click that link to bring up the record directly in CRM.

Step-by-Step Instructions

1. Go to any record in CRM. This could be a contact, account, opportunity, or other type of record.

2. Choose to either the **Copy a Link** or **E-mail a Link** option in the collaborate group of the ribbon.

3. The shortcut will either open in an Outlook e-mail message, or it will be copied to the clipboard.

Tips & Tricks

➤ Non-CRM users won't be able to view record shortcuts. Only users with a valid CRM login will be able to see your CRM records.

Bulk deleting records

You just got laid off, and you don't have anything to do until the end of the day. So why not delete your (now) former company's entire database? It's easy to do with a bulk delete. Best of all, there is no way to undo a bulk delete.

In all seriousness, this is a feature that should likely be turned off for most users, especially the ones you've laid off.

Bulk Record Deletion
Manage bulk record-deletion jobs.

Bulk Deletion Wizard   Help

This wizard helps you to delete selected records from selected entities/record types in Microsoft Dynamics CRM.

You will be asked to:
- Define deletion criteria for selected entity
- Select scheduling and notification options

To continue, click Next.

Back   Next   Cancel

Step-by-Step Instructions

1. On the **Navigation Pane,** click **Settings,** then **Settings,** and then **Data Management.**

2. Click **Bulk Record Deletion.**

3. Click the **New** button to create a new bulk deletion job.

4. Follow the instructions on the wizard to create a query of records to delete. Any records matching will be deleted.

Tips & Tricks

➢ Make sure you have a backup of any records before you bulk delete them.

➢ Be careful of this feature. If you don't specify a query, the bulk delete job will delete all records.

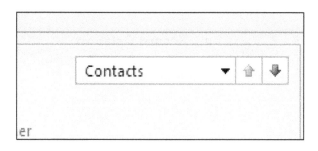

Scrolling through records on a form

Not a fan of huge list views? Would you prefer to scroll through record directly within a form?

In CRM, you don't need leave a form view to navigate between records. Instead, you can jump or scroll between records right within the form itself. Slick!

Step-by-Step Instructions

1. Open any record in your database.

2. In the top right corner of the form, you'll see a drop-down with the record name.

3. Click the drop-down to select a different record.

4. Click the arrow buttons to scroll through records

Tips & Tricks

➢ When you scroll through records this way, you can only view records from a single view and entity type.
➢ Only records in your current view are available or scrolling through.

View: **My Active Contacts**

Full Name

- Adrian Dumitrascu (sample)
- Brain LaMee (sample)
- Cat Francis (sample)
- Cathan Cook (sample)
- Darren Parker (sample)
- Eva Corets (sample)
- Forrest Chand (sample)
- Gabriele Cannata (sample)
- George Sullivan (sample)
- Marco Tanara (sample)
- Patrick Steiner (sample)
- Susan Burk (sample)
- Thomas Axen (sample)
- Yvonne McKay (sample)

Page 1

Viewing charts for a list

Lists are boring. They are long, confusing, and hard to interpret. If you want to decipher your data more easily, then simply create a chart from a list. This way, you'll spend less time trying to make sense of endless lists of data and more time selling.

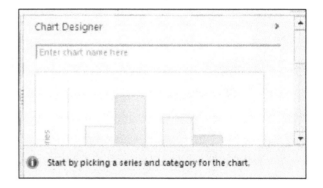

Step-by-Step Instructions

1. Go to any record list in CRM. This could be a contact, account, opportunity, or other type of record.

2. On the right, select the *Click here to view the chart* option.

3. A chart pane will appear on the right.

4. Configure your chart. It will automatically appear once you have defined it.

Tips & Tricks

➤ Once you leave a view the chart will disappear. If you want to use a chart often, you should check out dashboards, which are covered later in this book.

Using the Reading Pane

Are you a big fan of everything Outlook? Do you especially like that Reading Pane that allows you to both scroll through your e-mails and view them at the same time? Well, you're in luck. Now you can navigate through CRM records just like you would navigate through your Outlook e-mails.

Step-by-Step Instructions

1. Go to any record list in CRM. This could be a contact, account, opportunity, or other type of record list.

2. Click the **View** tab on the ribbon, and then the Reading Pane drop-down.

3. Select where you want the Reading Pane to appear.

Tips & Tricks

➤ You can only use the Reading Pane in Outlook 2010. You can't use this feature in Internet Explorer or older versions of Outlook.

Setting conditional formatting on a view

The world would be a boring place if everything looked the same. So would CRM. That's why you should set the conditional formatting on a view.

Setting conditional formatting allows you to configure records to be formatted in a certain way based on criteria. You could, for instance, have all opportunities of a certain amount show up bolded in the CRM list view.

Step-by-Step Instructions

1.   Click on an entity in the **Navigation Pane**, such as **Contacts**.

2.   Right-click on a column header in the list view, the select **View Settings.**

3.   Click the **Conditional Formatting** button and follow the instructions to create a rule-based format.

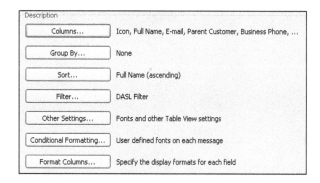

Tips & Tricks

> ➤ This feature is only available in Outlook 2010.
> ➤ This feature is also available in your personal Outlook contacts lists.

Installing the Outlook Social Connector

Social media is all the rage these days. If you're not using it in your business, get with it.

The Outl ook Social Connector allows you to display social media information within CRM. To install the connector, follow the steps below.

Step-by-Step Instructions

1. Point your web browser to http://tinyurl.com/osconnector to download the Social Connector for Outlook 2010. For older versions, search Bing to find the page.

2. Download and run the installation.

3. When Outlook opens, enter your username/password for participating social networking sites, like Facebook and Linkedin.

Tips & Tricks

➢ Once the Outlook Social Connector is installed, go to your list of CRM contacts in Outlook. Highlight a contact, and the social connector will automatically display a picture and recent activity from the social networking site.

Viewing social media information for a CRM contact

Once you've installed the Outlook Social Connector by following the steps on the previous page, you can view social media information for a contact in CRM.

The Outlook Social Connector pulls information about a CRM contact, such as pictures, from various social media profiles like LinkedIn.

Step-by-Step Instructions

1. Click on any contact from your list of CRM contacts in Outlook.

2. The Outlook Social Connector (assuming it is installed) will display recent page updates, pictures, and other information from various social networking sites.

Tips & Tricks

➢ Some social media information may only be available if you are friends with a contact on a social networking site.

Attaching SharePoint documents to a record

You can attach static documents to a CRM record. But that isn't very fun, is it? Attaching SharePoint documents to a record in CRM is really easy, and, lets be honest, you should be using SharePoint for document management if you have it.

1. Go to any record in CRM. This could be a contact, account, opportunity, or other type of record.

2. On the left **Navigation Pane**, click the **Documents** option.

3. In this area, you can add new documents for the record. You can also double-click a document to open it.

➢ You must first configure document management in the CRM Settings area, and you must have a SharePoint server in place to access SharePoint documents within CRM.

3

Using Activities

Tracking appointments and tasks in CRM ◆ *Using the Activities view in CRM* ◆
Viewing your calendar in CRM ◆ *Creating follow-up activities from a
record* ◆ *Creating a recurring activity* ◆ *Viewing pending activities and
past history associated with a record*

Tracking appointments and tasks in CRM

You already manage your tasks and appointments in Outlook, right? Luckily, your Outlo ok activities can be linked back to CRM records.

Tracking an appointment or task in CRM is similar to tracking a contact or e-mail. Just open an appointment and click the Set Regarding or Track buttons.

Step-by-Step Instructions

1. Go to your Outlook calendar or task list.

2. Locate an appointment or task and open it.

3. Click either the **Track** or **Set Regarding** buttons. (They're located on the ribbon.)

Tips & Tricks

➢ In general, you should use the Set Regarding button to relate tasks and appointments back to CRM records.

➢ If you are sending a meeting request, and if the recipient's email address matches up with a record in CRM, then you can just click the Track button.

Using the Activities view in CRM

Microsoft Dynamics CRM is much more than a fancy rolodex that keeps track of your contacts. It will also help you manage activities, such as phone calls, tasks, e-mails, letters, and appointments.

The activities view in Microsoft Dynamics CRM lets you work with activities that have been tracked in the CRM system.

1. On the **Navigation Pane**, click the **Workplace** option and choose **Activities**.

2. Use the filter at the top of the screen to set the activities you'd like to see.

3. Any changes made to activities in this view will sync to Outlook automatically.

➤   Think of this Activities view as a great way to create simple activity reports. You could, for example, bring up a list of all high priority tasks finished this week, and then you could export this list to Excel for PivotTable reporting.

Viewing your calendar in CRM

Calendars make your life a whole lot easier, even if they do give you a lot of work to d o. Using the calendar in Microsoft Dynamics CRM is simple and can help you visualize your schedule.

The calendar in CRM can be viewed by day, week, or month. Outlook activities show up in your CRM calendar if you track them in CRM.

Having said that, the Outlook calendar will give you a better user experience, so you'd likely be better off managing your calendar directly within Outlook.

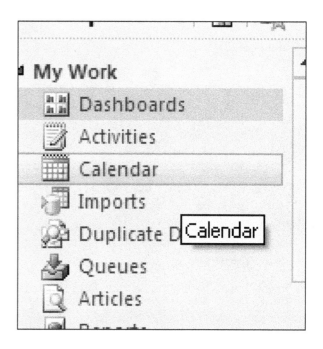

Step-by-Step Instructions

1. On the **Navigation Pane**, click the **Workplace** option and choose **Calendar**.

2. Your calendar will appear. From here, you can see your schedule, add new activities, and edit any activities that have been tracked to CRM.

Tips & Tricks

➢ This calendar view will *only* show activities that have been tracked in CRM. If you have any Outlook activities that aren't linked to CRM records, then you should ignore this view and work directly within Outlook.

Creating follow-up activities from a record

How would your customers feel if you never called them back? You may want to spare them any hard feelings by creating a follow-up activity. Follow-up activities can be created for any type of record, and it's really simple -- you will never even have to leave the form.

Any activity created using this method will be automatically associated with its record, and the activity will show up in your Outlook calendar.

1. Open a record. For example, you might open a company or contact record.

2. Click the **Add** tab of the ribbon. In the **Activity group** you will see the various activities you can create for this record.

3. A form assistant will appear on the right of the record. Enter details for your follow-up task or appointment and click Save.

➢ If you often create follow-up tasks for records, consider automating the process with a workflow. With the workflow feature, you can turn this whole process into a single click on the ribbon.

Creating a recurring activity

Tired of creating that activity over and over again? You don't need to! Simply create a recurring activity in CRM, and you won't have to worry about it again – unless you decide to delete it.

Step-by-Step Instructions

1. Click **Workplace** in the **Navigation Pane**, then **My Work**, and then **Activities**.

2. Click the Appointment drop-down, then select the Recurring Appointment option.

3. Configure your activity and click Save & Close.

Tips & Tricks

➢ You can only create a recurring appointment in CRM.

Viewing pending activities and past history associated with a record

You may remember what you've done with a contact or company in your database, but you may not be aware of the tasks and e-mails that others have done with a record.

In the Activities and History tabs within CRM, you can get a full picture of all activities, e-mails, and tasks that have been entered by anyone in your organization.

Step-by-Step Instructions

1. Open a record. For example, you might open a company or contact record.

2. On the left, click the **Activities** option.   A list of pending activities scheduled with the record will appear.

3. Now, click the **Closed Activities** option. This will show a list of e-mails sent, as well as past appointments and tasks that have been completed.

Tips & Tricks

➢ Using a sub-grid, you can add activities and history to the main screen on your record form.

4

Duplicate Detection

Scanning for duplicates ◆ *Merging duplicates* ◆ *Enabling duplicate detection in the system* ◆ *Modifying duplicate detection rules*

Scanning for duplicates

Believe it or not, mistakes can be made during data-entry. And duplicates are definitely annoying. And duplicates are definitely annoying.

Duplicate records in your database can cause you a lot of trouble, especially if they go unnoticed. Fortunately, Microsoft Dynamics CRM can help you automatically find duplicate records and deal with them.

Step-by-Step Instructions

1. Click on a list of records on the **Navigation Pane**, such as **Accounts**.

2. Click **Detect Duplicates** in the Records group of the ribbon.

3. Give the duplicate detection job a name, start time, and frequency. Click **OK**.

Tips & Tricks

➤ When creating a duplicate detection job, you have the option to narrow the job to a subset of the database. Setting a query in the duplicate detection wizard will narrow down the range of records searched. For example, you might only want to find duplicates that you own.

Merging duplicates

Have you found a duplicate record in your system? Rather than simply trashing one of the duplicate records, you should use the merging feature in Microsoft Dynamics CRM.

This feature gives you complete control over duplicate merging and is really easy to use. Duplicate records are lined up side by side so that you can decide which fields you want to keep in the merged record.

Step-by-Step Instructions

1. Find the two duplicate records. Hold Ctrl and click on each record. They should both be highlighted.

2. Click **Merge** in the Records group of the ribbon.

3. Highlight a master record. This should be the record that is more complete.

4. Click the radio button next to the field values that should be kept in the merged record.

Tips & Tricks

➢ Once you merge records, notes/histories/opportunities/etc from both records are combined.

➢ There is a checkbox at the bottom of the merge screen. It allows you to select all fields with data. It's a good idea to always click this box when merging duplicates. (You might have to scroll down to see it).

Enabling duplicate detection in the system

Why go through the trouble of dealing with duplicates when you can proactively keep them out of the database.

Configure Microsoft Dynamics CRM to automatically detect duplicates in the system, and then if you enter a record that is already in CRM, the system will warn you.

Step-by-Step Instructions

1. On the **Navigation Pane**, click **Settings** then **System**, and then **Data Management**.

2. Click **Duplicate Detection Settings**.

3. Choose to either enable or disable duplicate detection in the system.

Tips & Tricks

➤ Duplicate detection occurs when importing and also when adding new records to CRM.

➤ If you enable duplicate detection, make sure that your duplicate detection rules are fine tuned. (Check out the next page for info on the rules.)

Duplicate Detection Settings
Select default duplicate detection settings for your organization.

Duplicate Detection Settings
Select default duplicate detection settings for your organization.

Settings

Enable Duplicate Detection

☑ Enable duplicate detection:

    Detect duplicates:

      ☑ When a record is created or updated

      ☑ When Microsoft Dynamics CRM for Outlook goes from offline to online

      ☑ During data import

Help		OK	Cancel

Duplicate Detection Rules
Create, modify and publish duplicate detection rules.

▼ General
Name *
Status Reason *   Unpublished
Description

Duplicate Detection Rule Criteria
Base Record Type *   Matching Record Type
Case-sensitive   □

Field	Criteria	No. of Charact
Select		

Modifying duplicate detection rules

Duplicate detection has a built in set of rules, and while these might work well out-of-the-box, they might not be right for you.

Computers can do great things, but can't read your mind, and sometimes Microsoft Dynamics CRM will identify records as duplicates even though you want to keep them separate.

Step-by-Step Instructions

1. On the **Navigation Pane,** click **Settings,** then **System** and then **Data Management.**

2. Click **Duplicate Detection Rules.**

3. Click the **New** button to create a new duplicate detection rule.

Tips & Tricks

➢   The out-of-the-box rules might also not be strong enough. By default, CRM only identifies duplicate contacts as contacts with the same e-mail address.

➢   Adding additional rules (like a rule that finds contacts with the same last name and zip code) might yield more results in a duplicate detection job.

Finding Records

Finding records with the quick find feature ◆ Changing the fields that are searched during a Quick Find ◆ Running an Advanced Find ◆ Changing the columns that appear in Advanced Find results ◆ Saving an Advanced Find as a personal view ◆ Switching views (viewing recently visited views) ◆ Pinning a view ◆ Sharing your personal views with other users and teams ◆ Searching across entities

Finding records with the Quick Find feature

If you need to find a record quickly and easily, then Quick Find will be your friend. Sure, it may not be as clever as its big brother (the Advanced Find feature), but it's fast and simple so you'll be using it a lot.

If you need to find a contact by first/last name, you should use a Quick Find.

Step-by-Step Instructions

1. Click on a record type in the **Navigation Pane**. For example, you could click on **Contacts**.

2. You'll see a search field at the top of the record list.

3. Enter your search term into the field. Click the magnifying glass button or press Enter to execute the search.

Tips & Tricks

➤ The Quick Find feature searches on specific fields, but not all fields. To change the fields that are searched, follow the instructions on the next page.

➤ Use an asterisk (*) as a wild card. This is especially useful when searching for companies that begin with the word *The*.

Customize the System

Create, modify, or delete components in your organization. Components include entities, fields, relationships, forms, reports, processes, and others.

Changing the fields that are searched during a Quick Find

Quick Find is quick because it only searches certain fields. In each record type, Microsoft sets the fields that are searched during a Quick Find. If these default fields work for you, great!

If you aren't satisfied with your Quick Finds results, though, you can change the fields that are searched during a Quick Find.

Step-by-Step Instructions

1. Click **Settings** on the **Navigation Pane**, then **Customization**, and then click **Customizations**.

2. Click **Customize the System**.

3. On the left, click **Entities**, and then expand and entity.

4. On the left, click **Views**, and then double-click **Quick Find**.

4. Click **Add Find Columns** on the right. Check off any fields that you want to be searched and click OK.

5. Click **Save & Close**. Remember to publish your customizations.

Tips & Tricks

➢ Once you have added Quick Find views, click the Publish button to immediately enforce the changes.

Running an Advanced Find

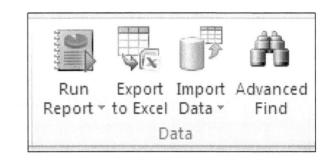

If you want to view a really specific data set, then you'll want to use Advanced Find. Running an Advanced Find is a bit more complicated than running a Quick Find, but it allows you more control over the search process. Advanced Find, for example, lets you search multiple fields at once.

An Advanced Find can also be saved as a view, so if you run a search often, this is likely your fastest option.

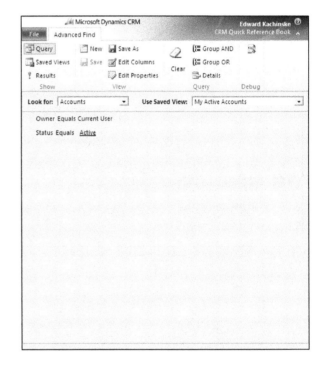

Step-by-Step Instructions

1. Click **Advanced Find** button in the Data group of the ribbon.

2. Choose an entity type from the drop-down.

3. Configure your query. (If in doubt, start by hovering your mouse over the Select text.

4. Click **Find**.

Tips & Tricks

➤ To customize the **default** set of columns that appear when you click the Find button, go to Settings | Customization | Customize your Solution. Double-click your record type and in the Views area, customize the Advanced Find view.

Changing the columns that appear in Advanced Find results

Have you run an Advanced Find but don't exactly like what you see? Then change the columns that appear in your Advanced Find results.

This can be especially useful if you want to perform a mail merge from an Advanced Find, as you can specify that you'd like to add fields like the address fields. Columns added will also appear in your view if you decide to save the Advanced Find as a view.

Step-by-Step Instructions

1. Click **Advanced Find** in the Data group of the ribbon.

2. Configure your query. (See the previous two pages).

3. Click **Edit Columns**. You can then add and remove columns.

4. Click **OK** and run the Advanced Find.

Tips & Tricks

➢ After clicking Edit Columns, use the green arrow buttons to move the order of columns.

➢ Double-click a column header to set its default width.

Saving an Advanced Find as a personal view

Do you ever find yourself running the same search over and over again? In Microsoft Dynamics CRM, you can save yourself from this hassle by saving your Advanced Find as a personal view.

Search results displayed in a saved view will be updated as your database changes. For example, if you save an Advanced Find that shows all current opportunities, the view will always give you the complete list of current opportunities. If you close an opportunity, it is removed from the view automatically.

Step-by-Step Instructions

1. Click the **Advanced Find** button on the toolbar.

2. Set up your query.

3. Click **Save As** in the ribbon.

4. Give your view a name.

5. Exit the Advanced Find.

6. Refresh. The Advanced Find should now show up in your list of views.

Tips & Tricks

➢ You can share the view with others. See the next page...

Switching views

Now that you have configured a custom view in your system, you'll need to know how to use it. Fortunately, switching between views is simple in CRM. Simply follow the directions below and you will be able to find those records in no time.

Step-by-Step Instructions

1. Click on a record type in the **Navigation Pane**. For example, you could click on **Contacts**.

2. You'll see a view drop-down at the top of the record list.

3. Click the drop-down and select a view.

Tips & Tricks

➤ To set a view as your default view, click the view tab, and then Set as Default View. This only works in Internet Explorer.

➤ In Outlook 2007 and 2010, views appear as tabs at the top of the view.

Pinning a view

Are you using Outlook and find yourself using the same views over and over again? By pinning a view in Outlook, you can keep multiple views open at the same time, and whenever you come back to that entity, your pinned views will automatically open.

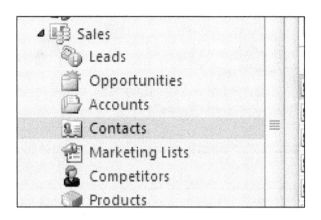

Step-by-Step Instructions

1. Click on a record type in the **Navigation Pane.** For example, you could click on **Contacts**.

2. You'll see views appear as tabs at the top of the record list.

3. Click on the pin icon on the view tab. This view is now pinned and will appear every time you open Outlook.

Tips & Tricks

➢ This feature is only available in Outlook 2007/2010.

➢ Click the pin icon again to unpin a view.

➢ Pinning a view only pins it for you. Other CRM users will not be affected.

Sharing your personal views with other users and teams

Have you just configured a nice new view that you think someone else in your organization could use? Well, quit hogging it! You are the only user who can see your personal views until you share them with another user or team.

1. Click **Advanced Find** in the Data group of the ribbon.

2. Click **Saved Views**.

2. Highlight the saved view. Click More Actions on the ribbon, then Sharing.

3. Add or remove users and click **OK**.

Tips & Tricks

➢ When sharing a view with others, you may want to restrict what they can do with the view. For example, sharing a view without giving someone Write access will ensure that they don't mess up the view.

Searching across entities

Most of the Advanced Find examples you'll run across will only involve one entity. So, you'll search for all contacts in Washington, DC. All opportunities greater than $50,000. And so on.

But let's say you want to search for all opportunities greater than $50K that are associated with an account in DC. That search requires searching across entities.

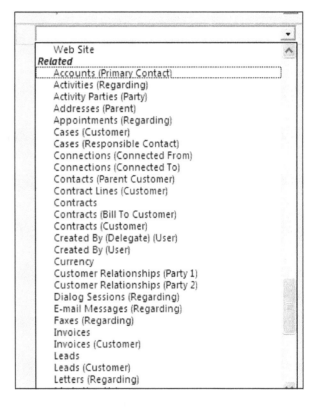

Step-by-Step Instructions

1. Click the **Advanced Find** button on the ribbon. For this example, let's assume that we are searching for opportunities.

2. Hover your mouse over the Select text. From the drop-down, scroll down the bottom of the list of fields. You'll see related entities. Following the example described above, you could choose Parent Customer (Account) to see a list of fields on the related account record.

Tips & Tricks

➢ "Customer" is a term in Microsoft Dynamics CRM that is used whenever a contact or account could be selected. For example, the Parent Customer of a contact could be either an account or contact record.

6

E-mail

Configuring Outlook e-mail settings

First thing's first: Unless your company has implemented the CRM E-mail Router, you'll need to configure Outlook e-mail to work with CRM.

This will allow Microsoft Dynamics CRM to send e-mails using CRM for Outlook. Why do you have to manually set Outlook to work with CRM for sending e-mail? Because Outlook basically assumes that all plugins are potentially harmful and requires that that you manually give CRM permission to send e-mails through Outlook.

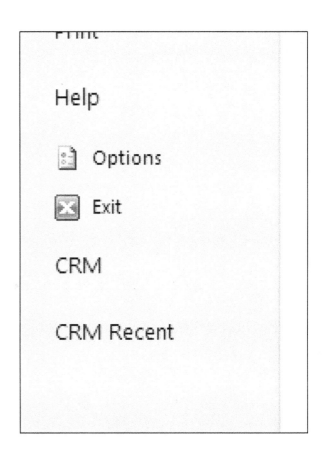

Step-by-Step Instructions

1. Click the **CRM** tab on the ribbon, and then **CRM**.

2. Click **Options**.

3. Click the **E-mail** tab.

4. Choose the option to allow CRM e-mails to be sent through Outlook and click OK.

Tips & Tricks

➢ If you don't allow Outlook to send e-mails on CRM's behalf, you will likely receive multiple annoying pop-up messages when CRM attempts to deliver e-mail messages.

➢ Each user must individually allow Outlook to send e-mail on behalf of CRM.

Installing the CRM E-mail Router

When you send an e-mail in CRM, that e-mail is either delivered through an individual user's Outlook program, or the e-mail is routed to the E-mail Router. This E-mail Router is a separate application that acts as a gateway between CRM and your Exchange/POP/SMTP e-mail server.

You can download the CRM E-mail Router from the Microsoft Dynamics CRM Resource Center.

Step-by-Step Instructions

1. Go to the Resource Center (It's at the bottom left corner of CRM in IE).

2. Under Downloads, Click Microsoft Dynamics CRM Online E-mail Router.

3. Click the Download button and follow the installation instructions.

Tips & Tricks

➤ The location of the download files for the E-mail Router may change. Do a Bing search if the instructions above don't work.

➤ The CRM E-mail Router only needs to be installed once per database. It will send emails for all of your users.

Sending a single e-mail from within Outlook

You can associate any Outlook e-mail (incoming or outgoing) with any record in CRM. If you have an important e-mail, tracking it in CRM will make it available to other CRM users, without sharing your entire Sent Items folder in Outlook.

Tracking e-mails back to records also makes it easier to gain a 360 degree understanding of your organization's interactions with a contact or company.

Step-by-Step Instructions

1. Create a new e-mail message in Outlook.

2. (Option 1) Click the **Track** button on the ribbon. Assuming the e-mail address for the recipient lines up with a record in CRM, the e-mail will be tracked to the record. (This may be a big assumption.)

3. (Option 2) Click the **Set Regarding** button if you want to manually associate the e-mail with a record in CRM

Tips & Tricks

➤ Tracked e-mails appear in the Closed Activities section for a record in CRM, alongside other completed activities.

Sending a single e-mail from within CRM

While you send most of your e-mail messages from within Outlook, you may at some point want to send a single e-mail from within CRM. Usually, this happens in cases when you already have a CRM record on the screen.

This way, you won't need to leave CRM to send an email, and it also gives you the opportunity to send e-mails from a computer that doesn't have Outlook on it.

Step-by-Step Instructions

1. (Option 1) Click New Activity on the toolbar, and then choose E-mail.

2. Fill out your e-mail and click **Send.**

3. (Option 2) Open a contact record and click the **Send Direct E-mail** button on the ribbon.

Tips & Tricks

➢ If you send e-mails directly from within CRM, you will need to have configured Outlook to send e-mails on CRM's behalf. Or your organization will need to have the CRM E-mail Router installed.

Creating a direct e-mail template

E-mail templates are really useful if you want to send the same e-mail to a bunch of recipients. E-mail templates can be set up and sent out directly in Microsoft Dynamics CRM.

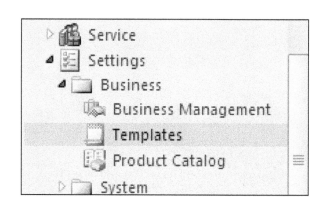

1. Click **Settings** on the **Navigation Pane**, then **Business**, and then click **Templates**.

2. Click **E-mail Templates**.

3. Click the **New** button on the Actions toolbar.

4. Select your template type (usually Contact or Account) and click OK.

5. Configure your template and click Save and Close.

➢ Click the Insert/Update button to insert field placeholders into an e-mail template.

➢ See the next page for instructions on what to do with e-mail templates once you have created them.

➢ For a better e-mail system, check out CoreMotives. More information is available at www.coremotives.com.

Sending a direct e-mail merge

Once you have your template ready, you can send an e-mail merge to a single person or a group of recipients directly in CRM.

Sending a direct e-mail is the quickest and easiest way to do an e-mail merge in Microsoft Dynamics CRM. (Other ways include using Workflow and using the Word mail merge feature.)

1. Highlight a group of records.

2. Click the **Direct E-mail** button in the **Collaborate** group of the ribbon.

3. Select an e-mail template, select a range of recipients, and click Send. (It's really that easy.)

➤ It's a good idea to send mass e-mails to a test group within your company before sending to the general population.

➤ If you are sending hundreds of emails (or more), then you should use a third party to deliver the messages. Sending through your Exchange server could end up putting your organization on spam blacklists.

Sending an e-mail merge using Word

So the direct e-mails sent within CRM are text only. If you want to insert fancy graphics, differing text sizes, or other HTML features, you'll need to send the e-mail using Microsoft Office Word.

Though an e-mail merge in word is harder to set up than a direct email (covered on the previous page) in CRM, you'll end up with a much more colorful end product.

Step-by-Step Instructions

1. Highlight a group of records.

2. Click **Merge** in the Collaborate group of the ribbon.

3. From the mail merge type drop-down, choose E-mail. Select a range of recipient records, and click OK.

4. Click **Open** to open the Word Document. Follow the instructions on-screen to create a template. The last step in the Word mail merge wizard will allow you to send the mail merge to e-mail recipients.

Tips & Tricks

➤ You cannot attach files to e-mails sent through this process. If you need to attach files, consider uploading them to a server and then reference them with a hyperlink.

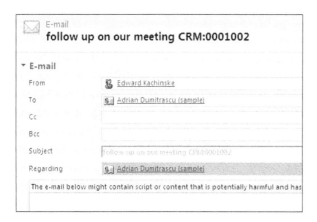

Viewing e-mails attached to CRM records

Once you've tracked an Outlook e-mail in CRM, you can view that e-mail under the associated record's closed activities. E-mails that are sent directly in CRM can also be viewed under a record's closed activities.

Tracking e-mails, of course, does have disadvantages. For example, if all of your messages are tracked, your boss will know whether or not you have been e-mailing prospects on a regular basis.

1. Open a record.

2. On the left, click **Closed Activities**.

3. In the date range drop-down, select a range of dates for history entries. The default only shows history entries for the last 30 days.

4. Double-click an e-mail history to open it.

➤ Attachments to e-mails will likely be available on history entries. Open a closed activities record, and then click the Attachments tab to see any files that were originally attached to the e-mail message.

Converting an e-mail

Did you just receive an e-mail from a promising customer? Don't waste time filling out an opportunity or lead form from that e-mail. Instead, simply convert that incoming e-mail to a CRM record in your system.

You can convert an e-mail to a lead, opportunity, or customer service case.

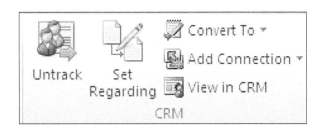

Step-by-Step Instructions

1. Highlight an e-mail in Outlook.

2. Click the **Convert To** drop-down in the CRM group of the ribbon.

3. Select a record type.

Tips & Tricks

➢ You can only convert an e-mail in Outlook 2010.

Sending contacts from Outlook to CRM

Chances are good that some people in your team have entered their important work contacts into their local Outlook contact list. Chances are also good that you have personal records in Outlook, too.

With CRM, you can choose which contacts get synchronized up into CRM. (So your dirty little secrets are safe in Outlook and won't go into CRM unless you click the Track button on them.)

Step-by-Step Instructions

1. In your local Outlook contacts list, locate the contact you'd like to sync with CRM. Highlight it.

2. Click **Track** on the ribbon.

Tips & Tricks

➤ Once tracked, changes made to a record in either CRM, Outlook, or your phone will sync throughout the system.

➤ When tracking an Outlook contact in CRM, you also have the option of linking the contact to an existing parent account in CRM.

➤ Contacts in Public Folders can't be synchronized with CRM. Only contacts in your local Outlook contacts list.

Tracking e-mails in CRM

You just extended a great offer to a customer, but Betty in accounting just sent them a cut-off letter because of late payments.

If everyone in your organization tracked e-mails in CRM, you would have seen Betty's e-mail in the contact's history. Tracking relevant e-mails is a great way to keep everyone in the loop on important correspondence.

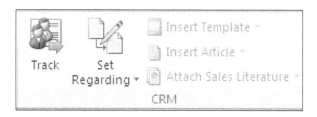

Step-by-Step Instructions

1. Create an e-mail message in Outlook.

2. At the top of the screen, click either the Track or Set Regarding buttons to track back to a CRM record.

3. Send the e-mail message. A copy of the message will show up in the record's closed activities list.

Tips & Tricks

➢   If you click the Track button, the system will track the e-mail message back to a contact or company using the e-mail address to find the appropriate record.

➢   Click the Set Regarding button if you want to choose a record for tracking the history.

7

CRM Mobile Express

Configuring CRM Mobile Express ◆ *Customizing Mobile Express forms* ◆
Accessing the database from your mobile phone

Configuring CRM Mobile Express

You can access your database anywhere, at any time using CRM Mobile Express. CRM Mobile Express is a CRM application that works on your cell phone. With CRM Mobile Express, you won't have any excuse to have a personal life. You can work all the time.

By configuring CRM Mobile Express, you will be able to customize which entities and forms show up when you access your CRM database from your phone.

Step-by-Step Instructions

1. Click **Settings** on the **Navigation Pane**, then **Customization**, then **Customizations** and then **Customize the System**.

2. Expand **Entities** and then click on the entity that you'd like to enable for mobile access.

3. If you would like this entity to be accessible on handhelds, check the Mobile Express for Microsoft Dynamics CRM option.

Tips & Tricks

➤ Some entities, like contacts, are enabled for access on CRM Mobile Express by default.

Customize the System
Create, modify, or delete components in your organization. Components include entities, fields, relationships, forms, reports, processes, and others.

Customizing Mobile Express forms

Phone screens are small, so you want to be selective when you configure what shows up on your Mobile Express forms. For example, you could probably wait until you find a computer to see a contacts anniversary date. Or not. That is the beauty of customizing the Mobile Express forms. You get to decide what shows up.

1. Click **Settings** on the **Navigation Pane,** then Customization, and then **Customizations.**

2. Expand **Entities**, and then expand the entity that you'd like to customize.

3. Select the Forms option on the left.

4. Open the mobile form and change the fields that display on the form.

➢ CRM Mobile Express is compatible with most current smartphones. iPhone, Palm Pre, Android, and just about any phone that has a finger push-screen will work with Mobile Express. Any mobile phone that supports javascript will work, which excludes many older Blackberry devices.

Accessing the database from your mobile phone

I'm sure you've thought to yourself, "I don't spend enough time working." Well, now you can access your database from the supermarket check-out line using CRM Mobile Express.

CRM Mobile Express is accessed in the browser of your cell phone. Basically, you just open a web browser on your phone and direct it to go to the URL for your database.

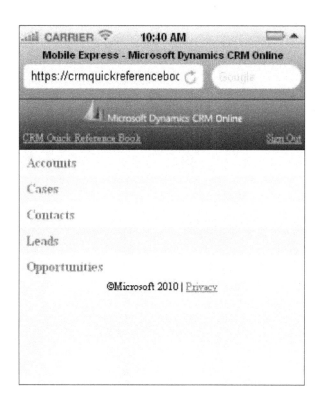

1. Open the browser on your phone.

2. Type your CRM database URL into the address bar.

3. Log in to your database with your Windows Live ID and password.

➢ Many Blackberry devices still don't support JavaScript, and if you have one of these devices, you may still be able to access your database using a third party application.

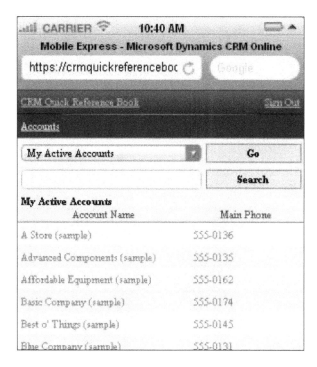

8

Using Leads

Entering a new lead ◆ *Qualifying a lead* ◆ *Disqualifying a lead*

Entering a new lead

A lead is a potential customer that you have not qualified yet. Think of leads as people on a spreadsheet, business cards left in a punchbowl at a conference. They're people without faces.

Once you know that the potential customer (1) has a pulse and (2) has expressed some interest in purchasing your product/service, then you should convert the person to a contact with a pending opportunity.

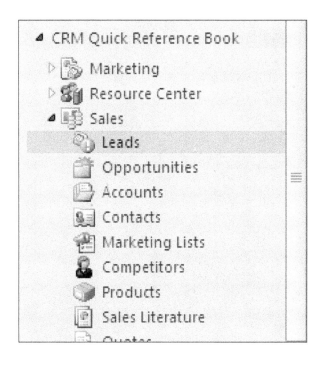

Step-by-Step Instructions

1. Click **Sales** on the **Navigation Pane**, and then click **Leads**.

2. Click **New** in the Records group of the ribbon.

3. Enter information about the lead. Click the **Save and Close** button.

Tips & Tricks

➢ Notes entered on a lead record will not transfer to a contact record when the lead is qualified. So if you are engaged enough with a lead to make notes, then it's time to convert the record to a contact.

➢ You may want to enter new contacts as leads and then convert them to contacts immediately. This way, you can enter information about the contact, company, and a pending opportunity all on one screen. This is generally easier than creating a separate company, contact, and opportunity record.

Qualifying a lead

A lead shouldn't remain a lead for long. Playing hard to get does not usually work very well in the sales world, so you will want to qualify a lead quickly.

As soon as you have made any kind of positive contact with a lead, you should convert it to a contact with an open opportunity.

Step-by-Step Instructions

1. Click **Sales** on the **Navigation Pane**, and then click **Leads**.

2. Double click the lead that you want to qualify.

3. Click **Qualify** on the ribbon.

4. Choose the **Qualify** option and click the option to create an Account, Contact, and Opportunity.

5. Click **OK**.

Tips & Tricks

➢ When a lead is qualified, the original lead record is deactivated and data from the lead is transferred to new account, contact, and opportunity records.

➢ When qualifying a lead, it might be a good idea to click the option to open the newly created contact, account, or opportunity records.

Disqualifying a lead

Sometimes leads don't work out, and that's OK. It's nothing you should take personally. Just disqualify that lead and move on. There are plenty of other fish in the sea.

A disqualified lead remains in the system, but not in your active views. If the customer ever re-surfaces, you can always re-activate the record.

Step-by-Step Instructions

1. Click **Sales** on the **Navigation Pane**, and then click **Leads**.

2. Double-click a lead.

3. Click **Qualify** on the ribbon.

4. Select the **Disqualify** option.

5. Click **OK**.

Tips & Tricks

➤ Disqualified records are automatically deactivated.

➤ To see a list of disqualified records, go to the Leads view and choose the Inactive Records view from the View drop-down in the upper right corner of the view.

9

Managing the Product Catalog

Creating unit groups

You're probably selling something, right? Fortunately, the product catalog in Microsoft Dynamics CRM can help you streamline the sales process and customize it for you or your business.

First you'll need to create unit groups. These are the units of whatever you are selling. Hours, for example, might be the unit that a service company works with. If you sell soda, your unit groups might be cans and cases.

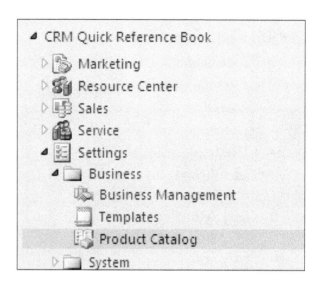

Step-by-Step Instructions

1. Click **Settings** on the **Navigation Pane**, then **Business** and then **Product Catalog**.

2. Click **Unit Groups**.

3. Click **New** on the ribbon.

4. Enter in a name and primary unit.

5. Click **Save and Close**.

 Unit Groups
A unit group contains the base unit a product is available in, such as a liter, and then lists all the different increments that this base unit is packaged for sale. For example, if the base unit is a two-liter bottle, then that product could be sold individually as a two-liter bottle or in a case containing 6 two-liter bottles. In this section, you create, manage, and delete units and unit groups in the product catalog.

Tips & Tricks

➤ If you are selling soda, you might have multiple unit groups. You might sell pallets, cases, and bottles of soda. Each could be units within a unit group.

Active Unit Groups

Search Active Unit Groups

Name	Categories
Default Unit	

Create Unit Group
You have chosen to add a new unit group to the product catalog. First, you specify the primary unit from which the other units will be derived.

Name *

Primary Unit *

OK   Cancel

Price Lists

A price list specifies what prices can be charged for each unit in the unit group of a product. In this section, you create, manage, and delete price list line items and price lists in the product catalog. You associate and disassociate products with price lists. You also specify various pricing options in the price list line items, such as the quantity selling option, the pricing method, and the rounding options.

Creating price lists

Once you have a unit group set up, you can create a price list. This list will help you determine and keep track of different prices for different customers.

You might, for instance, charge a different price for students, senior citizens, or government agencies. A price list can allow you to set different prices for different quantities of your product.

Step-by-Step Instructions

1. Click **Settings** on the **Navigation Pane**, then **Business** and then **Product Catalog.**

2. Click **Price Lists.**

3. Click **New** on the ribbon.

4. Give your price list a name and click **Save.**

5. Click **Add Price List Item.**

6. Enter in information about the item and click **Save and Close.**

Tips & Tricks

➤ Each product sold using CRM's product catalog will need to have a price associated with each price list.

➤ When you create a new opportunity, you'll have to specify a price list for the opportunity, and then when you add products to the opportunity, the customer's cost will be determined by the price list.

Adding products to the product catalog

You can't have a product catalog without products, so you'll need to know how to add products to you product catalog.

Managing your product catalog can be a little tricky, so just remember that the products in your product catalog are essentially just items that you sell.

Step-by-Step Instructions

1. Click **Settings** on the **Navigation Pane**, then **Business** and then **Product Catalog**.

2. Click **Products**.

3. Click **New** on the ribbon.

4. Enter in information about your product. Select a unit group and a default unit.

4. Click **Save**. In the details area, select the price list items associated with this product.

6. Click **Save and Close**.

Tips & Tricks

➢ Each product in the product list needs to have prices specified at each price list.

➢ If your opportunity process is fairly simple and doesn't involve huge inventory, using the product catalog might be overkill.

Products
A product is an item in the product catalog that you want to sell to your accounts. In this section, you add new products to and modify information for existing products in the product catalog. You activate or deactivate products, and also reclassify them to move them to other areas of the product catalog (and subject tree).

Managing discount lists

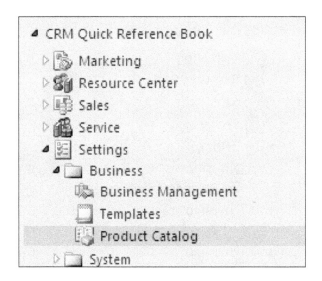

People are always looking to save money, so it would be really hard to sell a product if you never offered discounts.

Microsoft Dynamics CRM helps you keep track of the various discounts on your products with discount lists. You could have a senior citizen discount, a returning customer discount, or a discount associated with a specific promotion or discount code.

Discount Lists
A discount list contains the specific discounts that can be applied to a product, based on volume purchased. In this section, you create, manage, and delete discount lists in the product catalog.

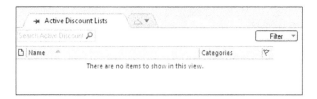

Step-by-Step Instructions

1. Click **Settings** on the **Navigation Pane**, then **Business,** and then click **Product Catalog**.

2. Click **Discount Lists**.

3. Click **New** on the ribbon.

4. Give your list a name and choose amount or percentage discount.

5. On the left, click **Discounts**.

6. Click **New Discounts**.

7. Enter in information about your discount.

8. Click **Save and Close**.

Tips & Tricks

➢ You can restrict the opportunity screens so that products can only be discounted by these pre-defined discounts.

10

Using Opportunities

Entering a new opportunity

So you've found potential sale? Good for you! You'll want to enter the potential sale into your database as an opportunity.

An opportunity is a record that contains information about a sale with a contact or account in your system.

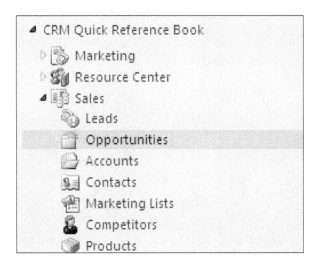

Step-by-Step Instructions

1. Click **Sales** on the **Navigation Pane**, and then click **Opportunities**.

2. Click **New** button in the Records group of the ribbon.

3. Enter information about your opportunity and click **Save and Close**.

Tips & Tricks

➢ When creating a new opportunity, you can add products from the product catalog by clicking the Products option on the left.

➢ An opportunity's dollar value can be automatically calculated based on the products selected and the price list chosen. Or, you can manually write-in a dollar amount.

Associating products with opportunities

Unless you skipped over Chapter 9, you know how to set up and manage you catalog. If you did skip it over, you might want to go back before reading this page.

Products in your product catalog can be associated with opportunities in your database, which helps you do important things like calculate potential revenue and create quotes. Plus, any product data that you add to an opportunity will transfer over to quotes, orders, and invoices.

Step-by-Step Instructions

1. Create or open an opportunity.

2. On the left, click **Line Items**.

3. Click **Add New Opportunity Product** in the ribbon.

4. Select a product, unit, and quantity.

5. Click **Save and Close**.

Tips & Tricks

➢ You must select a Price List on the opportunity before you can add any products to the opportunity.

➢ Pricing for products added to an opportunity will be calculated based on the price for the selected Price List.

Defining your competitors on an opportunity

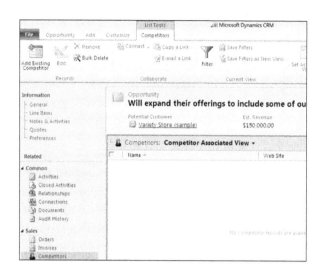

Keep your friends close and your enemies closer. Understanding your competition is an important part of sales and marketing, and with Microsoft Dynamics CRM, you can manage a list of competitors that will allow you to stay on top of whom you are winning (or losing) against.

Associate a competitor to an opportunity when find out that you are competing with a competitor for that opportunity.

Step-by-Step Instructions

1. Create or open an opportunity.

2. Click **Competitors** on the left.

3. Click **Add Existing Competitor** on the Actions Toolbar.

4. Highlight the competitor and click OK.

5. Click **Save and Close**.

Tips & Tricks

➤ When you close an opportunity, you'll also have the opportunity to select the competitor that you won/lost against.

Adding Sales Literature to a Product

Leaflets, sales slicks, price lists, galore! Keep this stuff handy in the Sales Literature feature, and you'll never have to go hunting for that price list again.

Sales literature can be associated with any product, and associating your sales literature will make easy for your salespeople to bring up product-specific documentation.

Step-by-Step Instructions

1. Click **Sales** on the **Navigation Pane**, and then click **Products**.

2. Open an existing product or click the **New** button to create a new product.

3. On the left, click **Sales Literature**.

4. Click **Add Existing Sales Literature** on the ribbon to link sales literature to this product.

Tips & Tricks

➤ If you need more complex document management, consider integrating SharePoint into your CRM database.

Attaching Sales Literature to outgoing e-mails

Sales literature doesn't just serve an internal purpose in your organization. It can also be attached to an e-mail. By doing this, your marketing and sales people can use sales literature documents when they conduct an e-mail campaign.

Step-by-Step Instructions

1. Open a new e-mail.

2. Click **Attach Sales Literature** drop-down, then select **More Sales Literature.**

3. Select your sales literature document and click **OK.**

Tips & Tricks

➢ To attach a sales literature document to an e-mail, you'll already need to have sales literature documents in you system. If you need help adding sales literature to CRM, see the previous page for instructions.

Look Up Record

Enter your search criteria and click Search to find matching records. Filter your results and view different columns of data by using the View options. Then, select the record you want and click Ok.

Look for: Sales Literature

View: Sales Literature Lookup View

Search: Search for records

Title	Type	
No Sales Literature records are available in this view.		

0 - 0 of 0 (0 selected)   ⊮ ◀ Page 1 ▶

New

Ok   Cancel

Organizing your opportunities

Opportunities can be hard to manage, especially if you have a lot of them. They are also an essential part of the sales process, so you will want to come up with a way to organize them so that you don't have this huge overwhelming list of opportunities to deal with.

You can get around this problem by creating views of certain opportunities. This way, you can have different views to view different types of opportunities.

Step-by-Step Instructions

1. Click **Sales** on the **Navigation Pane**, and then click **Opportunities**.

2. Click **Advanced Find** in the Data group of the ribbon.

3. Configure your Advanced Find to search for a subset of your opportunities.

4. Click the **Edit Columns** button to configure the columns that will appear in your view

5. Click the **Save As** button to save your Advanced Find as a view on the opportunity screen.

Tips & Tricks

➢ Check out the Search chapter of this book for more information on the Advanced Find feature.

Closing a won or lost opportunity

Eventually you will either win or lose a sales opportunity. When this time comes, you will want to close the won or lost opportunity.

Opportunities are no longer active once they have been closed and do not appear with your active contacts. But fear not! Any close/lost opportunity can be reactivated if the customer comes back.

Step-by-Step Instructions

1. Double-click an opportunity in the opportunity list view.

2. Click **Close as Won** or **Close as Lost** in the Actions group of the ribbon.

3. Define the opportunity as won or lost and choose a reason for the end of the opportunity.

4. Enter in any other important information.

5. Click **OK**.

Tips & Tricks

➤ For sales reports that show won/lost/inactive opportunities, consider creating a pivot table in Excel.

11

Quotes, Orders, and Invoices

Creating a quote from an opportunity ◆ *Modifying pricing and products on a quote* ◆ *Activating a quote* ◆ *Printing a quote* ◆ *Generating n order from a quote* ◆ *Generating an invoice from an order* ◆ *Integrating with Microsoft Dynamics GP*

Creating a quote from an opportunity

So an opportunity is finally interested in your product? The next step in the sales process involves sending a quote to the potential customer.

Quotes in Microsoft Dynamics CRM are automatically generated as a Word Document.

Step-by-Step Instructions

1. Open an existing opportunity.

2. Click **Quotes** on the left.

3. Click **Add New Quote** on the ribbon.

4. Make sure the sales information is correct. (It will pull product information from the opportunity into this quote.

5. Click **Save and Close**.

Tips & Tricks

➢ For advanced quoting with CRM 4.0, check out Experlogix. www.experlogix.com

Modifying pricing and products on a quote

When you create a quote, you are given the option to modify the pricing and products on the quote. You might, for example, want to enter in extra products or change the pricing of a product in your quote.

These changes will show up in the quote but not the parent opportunity.

Step-by-Step Instructions

1. Create a new quote from an opportunity.

2. Save the quote.

3. On the left, click **Products**, and then click **Add New Quote Product** on the ribbon.

4. Enter in your pricing and product information.

5. Click **Save and Close**.

Tips & Tricks

➢ If you have complex quoting requirements, you may need to do much of your quoting in your accounting system. Links to Quickbooks, Microsoft Dynamics GP, Microsoft Dynamics NAV, and others are all available. (And the Microsoft ones are generally free!)

Activating a quote

Have you created and modified your quote to your liking? Before you send it off to a customer, you will want to activate your quote.

Once activated, the quote will be set to read-only in the system. If you need to change anything in the quote after you've reactivated it, you should create a new quote from the opportunity.

Step-by-Step Instructions

1. Open a quote.

2. Click **Activate Quote** in the Actions group of the ribbon.

Tips & Tricks

➢ Invoices can only be generated from an activated quote.

➢ You should activate your quote before you print it. (Instructions for printing the quote are on the next page.)

Printing a quote

Once you have made sure that all of the information in your quote is correct, you'll want to print it. Quotes in Microsoft Dynamics CRM are automatically generated as a Word document

Step-by-Step Instructions

1. Create a quote for an opportunity.

2. Click **Print Quote for Customer** on the **Actions** section of the ribbon.

3. A Word document will open. Verify the information and print the document.

Tips & Tricks

➢ You may want to edit the template that CRM uses for quotes. Go to Settings | Templates to see the mail merge templates that can be edited.

➢ In Word 2010, you can save the Word document directly as a PDF file, which is useful if you don't want the customer to be able to edit the quote.

Generating an order from a quote

So a customer has received your quote and decided to buy your product. You're almost there. The heavy lifting has been done, and you now have to fulfill the order.

In CRM, you can generate an order from any activated quote. Creating an order shows the system that your customer has accepted the quote, and it will tell your fulfillment department that there is an order ready to ship.

Step-by-Step Instructions

1. Open a quote.

2. Click **Activate Quote** on the ribbon.

3. Click the **Create Order** on the ribbon.

Tips & Tricks

➤ Once you create an order for a quote, you should go back and close your originating opportunity. Mark it as having been won.

Create Order
Use this quote to create an order.

Quote ID: QUO-01001-P5S3N5   Revision ID: 0

Status Reason   Won

Date Won   2/18/2011

Description

○ Close Opportunity

Actual revenue is: ○

◉ Calculated from quotes

◉ Don't update opportunity

OK   Cancel

Generating an invoice from an order

Hang in there, because there's one last step in the opportunities / quotes / orders / invoices process. Your customer will need an invoice from you once an order is placed.

This feature is really only useful if CRM is automatically integrated into your accounting system.

1. Open an order.

2. Click the **Create Invoice** on the ribbon.

➢ If your CRM system is not integrated into your accounting system, then you may set up a workflow to automatically send your accounting department an e-mail whenever an invoice is created in CRM. This way, they'll know to send the customer a bill.

Integrating with Microsoft Dynamics GP, AX, and NAV

I know, you're not an accountant, and you didn't get CRM to make your life more complicated. But integrating accounting programs like GP, AX, and NAV can be very useful. And it's pretty easy, so you might as well do it.

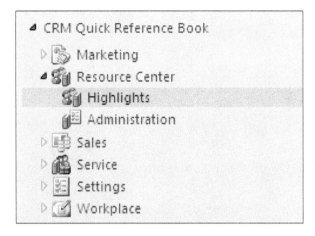

Step-by-Step Instructions

1. Log into CustomerSource, where you can download the Connector for Microsoft Dynamics CRM.

2. Install the Connector for Microsoft Dynamics CRM. You will likely need help from your GP and CRM partners to connect the two systems.

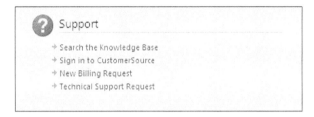

Tips & Tricks

➢ The easiest way to log into CustomerSource is through CRM. Log into your CRM database in Internet Explorer and click the Resource Center in the bottom left corner of the screen. From the Resource Center, you'll find a link to CustomerSource.

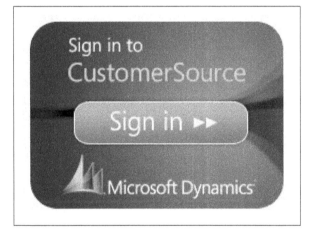

12

Marketing Lists

Creating a static marketing list ◆ *Adding members from a list view* ◆ *Using lookup or Advanced Find to add members* ◆ *Using Advanced Find to remove or evaluate members* ◆ *Modifying the list membership view* ◆ *Creating a dynamic marketing list* ◆ *Viewing marketing list information for a single record*

Creating a static marketing list

It's time to learn how you can use Microsoft Dynamics CRM to convince your potential customers that they should buy from you.

Before you begin marketing, you will want to create marketing lists so that you can target specific groups of records with campaigns. With a static marketing list, you add and remove members manually.

Step-by-Step Instructions

1. Click **Marketing** on the **Navigation Pane**, and then click **Marketing Lists**.

2. Click **New** button in the Records group of the ribbon.

3. Name your marketing list. Then choose a member type (either contact, account, or lead) and add any other important information.

4. Click **Save and Close**.

Tips & Tricks

➢ Marketing lists can be made up of either contacts, accounts, or leads. If you need a marketing list that has both contacts and leads, for example, you'd have to create two separate marketing lists.

Look Up Record

Enter your search criteria and click Search to find matching records. Filter you results and view different columns of data by using the View options. Then, select the record you want and click OK.

Look for: Marketing List ☐ Show Only My Records

View: Basic Marketing Lists

Search: Holiday Card ✕

	Name	Type	Purpose
☑	Holiday Card	Static	

1 - 1 of 1 (1 selected)   ⏮ ◀ Page 1 ▶

Properties   New

OK   Cancel   Remove Value

Adding members from a list view

A marketing list without records is about as useful as an empty paper bag. Adding records to a marketing list is really easy, so you'll soon have lots of people and companies in your marketing lists.

It may be easiest to add records from a list view. This way, you can just highlight a few contacts, accounts, or leads – and then you're only two clicks away from dumping them into a marketing list.

Step-by-Step Instructions

1. In a list view, highlight a group of records.

2. Click **Add** to **Marketing List** in the **Collaborate** group of the ribbon.

3. Select a marketing list and click OK.

Tips & Tricks

➢ Use CTRL + CLICK in any list view to highlight multiple non-consecutive records.

➢ Use SHIFT + CLICK in any list view to highlight multiple consecutive records.

Using lookup or Advanced Find to add members

Advanced Find or Lookup can also be used to add members to a marketing list. This is really useful if you want a specific type of record to be added to your marketing list.

It can also be useful if you need to add more than just a few records to a marketing list. For example, if you need to add all 2,000 contacts in Montana to a marketing list, you'd want to use Advanced Find to add these people to your list.

Step-by-Step Instructions

1. Open a marketing list.

2. Click **Marketing List Members** on the left.

3. Click **Manage Members** on the ribbon.

4. Select either lookup or Advanced Find. Click OK.

5. You will be able to perform a lookup of records that will be pulled into the marketing list.

Tips & Tricks

➤ There is no easy way to undo the addition of records to a marketing list.

Using Advanced Find to remove or evaluate members

Do you have a record in your marketing list that isn't even worth dealing with? You can remove any record like this from your marketing list.

Let's say you want to remove all contacts in Montana from a marketing list. Using this procedure makes the mass removal simple.

1. Open a marketing list.

2. Click **Marketing List Members** on the left.

3. Click **Manage Members** on the ribbon.

4. Choose to run an Advanced Find.

5. Highlight the contacts from the resulting Advanced Find Results screen that you want to remove and click the **Remove from Marketing List** button.

➤ Again, there's no way to undo this action. So make sure you want to remove these records from a list before you start.

Modifying the list membership view

When you open a marketing list and look at the list of contacts, accounts or leads that are currently in the list, you can export this list easily to Excel. That's the good news.

When looking at a list of group members, you can switch views to see different configurations of columns. This is especially useful if you need to export a list of group members to Excel.

Step-by-Step Instructions

1. Open a group.

2. Click the **Marketing List Members** option on the left.

3. From the view drop-down, click **Create Personal View**.

4. Give your personal view a name, and click the **Edit Columns** button to specify the columns that should appear in the view.

Tips & Tricks

➢ Click the Export to Excel button on the toolbar to export your list members (and the columns defined in the view).

Creating a dynamic marketing list

A dynamic marketing list is a marketing list based on specific criteria. Does that sound like Greek to you? Put simply, a dynamic marketing list is based on an Advanced Find query.

Step-by-Step Instructions

1. Click **Marketing** on the **Navigation Pane**, and then **Marketing Lists**.

2. Click **New** in the Records group of the ribbon.

3. Give your list a name, member type, and select Dynamic as your marketing list type.

4. Click **Manage Members** on the ribbon. A new Advanced Find query will pop up.

Tips & Tricks

➤ You can't manually add or remove members to a dynamic marketing list. Instead, the list is managed automatically based on the Advanced Find that you set up.

Viewing the marketing list information for a single record

Do you want to check whether or not a record has been added to a marketing list? Want to keep track of which marketing lists a certain record belongs to. Fortunately, marketing lists for a single record can be easily viewed when you open a contact, account, or lead.

Step-by-Step Instructions

1. Open a record. (Either a contact, account, or lead record.)

2. On the left, click **Marketing Lists.**

3. A list of marketing lists that the current record belongs to will appear.

Tips & Tricks

> When viewing list membership for a contact, account, or lead record, you can click the Add to Marketing List button.

13

Mail Merge

Running a mail merge with Word ◆ *Printing labels for records* ◆ *Saving your mail merge template as an organization or personal template* ◆ *Recording a history of letters sent on individual records*

Running a mail merge with Word

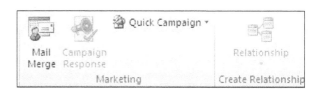

Mail merge in Microsoft Word is a great tool that can help your organization give a personalized touch. Because let's face it: In a business context, giving the perception of a personalized touch is more valuable than actually sitting down and touching each mail piece personally.

Mail merge in Microsoft CRM is best done using Microsoft Office Word, so you won't have to change your existing business process.

Microsoft Dynamics CRM Mail Merge for Microsoft Office Word
Select the options for this mail merge.

Select the mail merge type:
[Letter]

Start with a:
- Blank document
- Organization mail merge template
- Personal mail merge template

Merge:
- Selected records on current page
- All records on current page
- All records on all pages

Select data fields:
To select the data fields to use with this mail merge, click Data Fields.
[Data Fields]

[OK]   [Cancel]

Step-by-Step Instructions

1. Highlight any records that you want to be included in your mail merge.

2. Click **Mail Merge** in Add tab of the Ribbon.

3. Select a mail merge type, a template, and a merge range of records.

4. Click **OK**. A Word document will open directly to the Word mail merge wizard.

5. Complete the wizard to run your mail merge.

Tips & Tricks

➢ At the end of the mail merge, the system will prompt you to upload your template into the CRM system. This is a good idea if you will run a similar letter in the future.

Printing labels for records

You don't actually print out labels by hand, do you? If you do, then you're a couple of decades behind the times and should be using mail merge to create labels for your records.

Printing labels is best done in Word, just like most of the other mail merges that you will do. Word is compatible with most sheet-fed label types, including Avery Labels.

Step-by-Step Instructions

1. Highlight a list of records. (Or go to a view that contains your records. Or perform an Advanced Find of the records for whom you'd like to print labels.)

2. Click **Mail Merge** in Add tab of the Ribbon. Select Labels from the drop-down.

3. Either select to use an existing template or create a mail merge from a blank document.

4. Click **OK**. A Word document will open, and it will open directly to the Word mail merge wizard.

Tips & Tricks

➤ Before printing your labels, it's a good idea to scan through them to make sure that all of the formatting (especially with foreign addresses) is correct.

Saving your mail merge template as an organization or a personal template

In Microsoft Dynamics CRM, you can save a mail merge template either as a personal template or an organizational template. The difference between the two has to do with ownership: personal templates are only available to you, while organizational documents are available to everyone.

Note: At the end of running a mail merge, you'll have the option to upload the template to CRM. That may be easier than the instructions on this page.

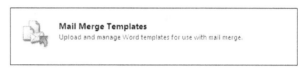

Step-by-Step Instructions

1. Click **Settings** on the **Navigation Pane**, then **Business,** and then click **Templates**.

2. Click the **New** button on the Actions toolbar.

3. Enter in important information about your template. Then click browse and locate the XML template file that you want to use.

4. Click **Attach**. This template will be saved as a personal template.

5. Click **Settings** on the Navigation Pane, then **Business**, and then click **Templates**.

6. Highlight the template. Click More Actions, then Make Available to Organization.

Recording a history of letters sent to individual records

It's important to keep a history of all of the mail merges that you run. Otherwise you might send the same one multiple times, and that wouldn't look very professional.

When you print a mail merge, you are given the option to create a history of the merge.

1. Follow the mail merge process.

2. When you print the final merged document, you will be prompted to create a history.

➤ If you forget to create a history, print the document again to XPS or PDF, and you'll get the prompt to create a history of the sent

14

Using Quick Campaigns

Scheduling a call with multiple records ◆ *Running a Quick Campaign for marketing list members* ◆ *Viewing Quick Campaigns after they have been initiated*

Scheduling a call with multiple records (Quick Campaigns)

Are you having trouble keeping track of all of those different customers that you should be calling? Is your workstation overwhelmed with white sticky notes with phone numbers and times written on them? Should you call everyone from the trade show last week?

Microsoft Dynamics CRM allows you to schedule a call with multiple records. Phone calls scheduled in CRM will appear in Outlook as tasks.

Step-by-Step Instructions

1. Highlight a group of records, like contacts, leads, or accounts.

2. Click the **Create Quick Campaign** in on the Add tab in the Marketing group of the ribbon.

3. Give your quick campaign a name and click **Next**.

4. Select Phone Call and click **Next**.

5. Specify content of the activity and click **Next**.

6. Click **Create**. A phone call for each highlighted record will be created, and this record will sync with Outlook.

Running a Quick Campaign for marketing list members

Quick Campaigns are kind of like Campaigns, but they only have one campaign activity.

Running a Quick Campaign for bunch of marketing list members is a lot more efficient than going through your entire database and individually selecting records to add to your quick campaign.

Step-by-Step Instructions

1. Click **Marketing** in the **Navigation Pane**, and then click **Marketing Lists**.

2. Double-click a marketing list.

3. Click **Create Quick Campaign** on the Add tab of the ribbon.

4. Give your **Quick Campaign** a name and click **Next**.

5. Select the type of activity you'd like to create for your quick campaign and choose who will own these activities.

6. Add specific information for the type of activity that will be created and click Next. This activity (either a task, e-mail, letter, etc.) will be created for each marketing list member.

Viewing Quick Campaigns after they have been initiated

Need to check up on that Quick Campaign after it has been created? Not quite sure whether your configured it correctly?

Fortunately, Quick Campaigns can be easily viewed after they have been initiated.

Step-by-Step Instructions

1. Click **Marketing** on the **Navigation Pane**, and then click **Quick Campaigns**.

2. Double-click a **Quick Campaign**. Here, you can see activities created from the quick campaign, campaign responses, a list of recipients for the campaign, and more.

Tips & Tricks

➤ If you have a complex campaign in the works that involves multiple e-mails, letters, or other marketing activities, consider creating a full campaign instead of a quick campaign.

15

Using Campaigns

Creating a campaign or campaign template ◆ *Adding marketing lists to a campaign* ◆ *Adding planning tasks to a campaign* ◆ *Adding campaign activities* ◆ *Adding campaign responses*

Creating a campaign or campaign template

Campaigns are central to the marketing process. They allow you to organize a bunch of marketing activities together under a single campaign.

In Microsoft Dynamics CRM, you can either create a campaign or a campaign template. A campaign template will allow you to save and reuse a particular campaign's structure and apply it to other campaigns.

Step-by-Step Instructions

1. Click **Marketing** on the **Navigation Pane**, and then click **Campaigns**.

2. Click the **New** template button on the Actions toolbar.

3. Enter in a name for the campaign template.

4. Add planning tasks and marketing activities to the template.

5. Click **Save and Close**.

Tips & Tricks

➤ An example of where you'd use a campaign template: Let's say that four times a year, you do a customer renewal campaign. Create this campaign as a template, and then your planning tasks and marketing are easily replicated into each new campaign.

Adding marketing lists to a campaign

A campaign that targets a specific group of records would be much more successful than a campaign that targets an entire database.

Adding a marketing list to a campaign will give you a high level of control over who is targeted by your campaign. If you're targeting more than one type of record (like, for example, if you're targeting both current contacts and leads) then you'll need to have multiple marketing lists associated with your campaign.

Step-by-Step Instructions

1. Open a marketing campaign.

2. On the left, click **Target Marketing Lists.**

3. Click **Add Existing Marketing List** on the ribbon.

4. Check any marketing lists that you want to include in the campaign. Click **OK.**

Tips & Tricks

➢ A holiday mailer is a good example of a campaign that could have multiple marketing lists. You might have one list for people who should get a card an another list for people who should get a present.

Adding planning tasks to a campaign

Careful planning is the key to the success of a campaign. If you are planning a substantial campaign, such as a charity event, you will need some kind of resource that helps you to keep track of the internal tasks that you and your organization need to complete.

Adding planning tasks in Microsoft Dynamics CRM will help you manage various internal tasks, and it will also help you evaluate whether the effort to launch the campaign was worth the monetary result.

Step-by-Step Instructions

1. Open a campaign.

2. On the left, click **Planning Tasks.**

3. Click **New**.

4. Fill in information about your planning task and click save and close.

5. Repeat this process until all planning tasks are in the system.

Tips & Tricks

➢ Examples of planning tasks include: buying stamps, licking envelopes, printing labels, designing postcards, getting executive approval for artwork and text copy, internal meetings to cover strategy, etc.

Adding campaign activities

Campaign activities are the bulk of your campaign. Any activity, like a phone call or e-mail, can be added to a campaign in Microsoft Dynamics CRM. You can even add a mail merge to as a campaign activity.

Campaign activities are the activities that involve some level of direct interaction with your customer.

Step-by-Step Instructions

1. Open a campaign.

2. On the left, click **Campaign Activities**.

3. Click **Add New Campaign Activity** button on the ribbon.

4. Enter information about the activity. Click **Save and Close**.

5. Repeat this process until all campaign activities are entered into your system.

Tips & Tricks

➤ Examples of campaign activities include: Sending a postcard, sending an e-mail blast, engaging a telemarketing effort, sending out a survey, inviting people to an event, and so on.

Adding campaign responses

Do you want to know if all of your hard work on a marketing campaign has paid off? Campaign responses help you determine how effective a particular campaign is.

Adding campaign responses manually is pretty painful. Most people set up systems to automate the creation of these campaign responses, either through third-party add-on products or through the built-in Workflow feature.

Step-by-Step Instructions

1. Open a campaign.

2. On the left, click **Campaign Responses**.

3. Click **Add New Campaign Response** on the ribbon.

4. Enter in any important information about your campaign response.

5. Click **Save and Close**.

Tips & Tricks

➤ If you integrate a third party e-mail system like CoreMotives or ExactTarget, then each read/open/click on an outgoing e-mail will be recorded in the system as a campaign response.

16

Using Cases

Creating a customer service case ◆ *Assigning a knowledge base article to a case*
◆ *Adding case notes and activities* ◆ *Deleting or canceling a case* ◆ *Resolving a
case* ◆ *Managing service queues*

Creating a customer service case

While we all sometimes wish we could ignore our customers after a sale has been made, businesses that thrive are usually those with strong post-sales customer service.

It's easy to create and manage your service cases in Microsoft Dynamics CRM. Managing incidents in CRM will help your service techs keep track of all of the work that they need to do.

Step-by-Step Instructions

1. Click **Service** on the **Navigation Pane**, and then click **Cases**.

2. Click in the Records group of the ribbon.

3. Enter in important information about your service case. Click **Save and Close**.

Tips & Tricks

➢ If you require that customers who call for service have an active contract in place, you can link these cases to contract and contract lines.

➢ Each contract line within a contract allows the customer to have either a certain number of incidents or a certain number of minutes.

Assigning an article to a case

Articles help you keep track of all of the technical information that is needed for service requests.

Things like FAQs, how-tos, and bug-fixes are all examples of articles. They can be assigned to a particular service case for quick reference.

Step-by-Step Instructions

1. Open a service case.

2. Click the **Notes and Articles** form section.

3. Under **Knowledge Base**, click **Lookup**.

4. Search for your article.

5. Select the article and click **OK**.

Tips & Tricks

➢ Only one article can be linked to each service case in CRM. If more are required, you may just enter the article numbers in the case notes.

➢ If the word "Case" doesn't fit your business, you could change the name of cases to Incidents, Complaints, or something more appropriate. This is done in Settings | Customization | Customize the System.

Adding case notes and activities

Any time you create a case in the system, you'll need to add case notes (and sometimes activities) to complete the record of contact with the customer.

You've probably been on the phone with a phone company or big corporation where the support technician had to look at your notes to see what the last technician had done with your account.

1. Open a service case.

2. Click the **Notes and Articles** form section.

3. Click in the space provided to add a new note for this case. When you are finished, click outside of the notes area to see that your name and the current date have been appended to the note.

3. Click the **Follow-up** button on the toolbar to add a follow-up task or appointment linked back to the case.

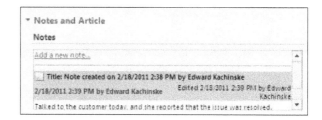

Tips & Tricks

➢ In Outlook, you can also link an appointment or task back to a specific task. Open the activity and click the Set Regarding button on the ribbon. In the record type drop-down, choose Cases.

Deleting or canceling a case

Did you accidentally enter a case into the system and then realize that no case was really needed? Then delete it out of the system, and you will never have to think about it again.

If a customer calls to cancel a customer service incident, you can also cancel it.

Step-by-Step Instructions

1. Open a service case.

2. Click **Delete** in the Save group of the ribbon.

3. Click **Cancel Case** in the Actions group of the ribbon.

Tips & Tricks

➢ Deleting a case permanently removes it from the system. Once deleted, there is no option to undelete the record.

➢ Canceling a case sends the case into a canceled status.

Resolving a case

Eventually, you'll hit a point where you will successfully resolve a case.

If you have helped a customer successfully, then you will want to resolve the case ASAP. You wouldn't want other technicians working on one of your resolved cases, would you?

Step-by-Step Instructions

1. Open a case.

2. Click **Resolve Case** in the Actions group of the ribbon.

3. Enter in any important information about your case and click **OK**.

Tips & Tricks

➤ If you resolve a case and then realize that the issue wasn't actually resolved, you can reactivate a resolved case. Just go to your list of resolved cases and open the case. From the ribbon, you'll be able to reactivate the case.

➤ You should probably create workflow alongside the resolution of cases in CRM. So, when a customer service case is resolved, an e-mail could automatically go out to the end customer to let him/her know that the issue has been resolved.

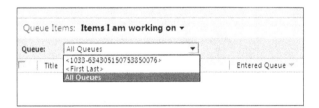

Managing service queues

If you have more than one customer service representative, you'll probably want to have a queue to manage distribution of cases within your support department. Cases can be assigned to a queue, and then the next available rep can accept the cases that best fit their skill sets.

If you see a case in a service queue that you want to take on, accept it, and it will be assigned to you.

Step-by-Step Instructions

1. Click **Settings** on the **Navigation Pane**, then Business, and then click **Business Management**. (Or click on **Workplace** and then **My Work**.)

2. Click **Queues**.

3. Click the **New** button to create a new queue.

Tips & Tricks

➢ Cases that you have accepted will appear in your In Progress queue

17

Service Contracts

Creating a service contract template ◆ *Creating a contract from a template* ◆ *Adding contract lines to a contract* ◆ *Linking service cases to a contract* ◆ *Invoicing a contract* ◆ *Copying/renewing a contract.*

Creating a service contract template

Service contracts are important for your business because they help you manage the various service options that you offer your customers. They also enforce paid service engagements.

Before you begin creating service contracts, you need to create a contract template, which acts as a mold for your various service contracts.

1. Click **Settings** on the **Navigation Pane**, then **Business,** and then click **Templates.**

2. Click **Contract Templates.**

3. Click the **New** button on the toolbar.

4. Enter in information about your contract template, such as the name or the allotment type.

5. Click **Save and Close.**

➢ Service contacts can have two types of allotments: incidents or minutes. A support contract could offer a certain number of minutes as its deliverable, or it could offer a certain number of calls/incidents.

Contract Templates
Create and manage custom templates for contracts.

Creating a contract from a template

Have you created a contract template? Then you are ready to create an actual service contract from that template. This service contract will contain the service agreement between you an actual customer.

It's important to note that the contract itself does not actually offer any specific deliverables to your customer. That comes with contract lines, which are covered on the next page.

Step-by-Step Instructions

1. Click **Service** on the **Navigation Pane**, and then click Contracts.

2. Click **New** in the Records group of the ribbon.

3. Choose the template for your service contract.

4. Give your contract a name, customer, start/end date, bill-to name, and any other information.

5. Click the **Save** button.

Tips & Tricks

➢ You won't be able to link any cases to this service contract until the contract has been invoiced.

➢ This contract will only be valid between the start/end dates. Outside of these dates, the contract will be invalid.

Adding contract lines to a contract

Once you have a contract set up, you need to add contract lines to add the details of the contract.

Think of contract lines as the individual deliverables that make up the service contract. If you were a plumber, for instance, you might have a contract line designating a certain number of service visits to an office building.

1. Open a contract.

2. On the left, click **Contract Lines**.

3. Click **Add New Contract** Line on the ribbon.

4. Enter in information about your contract line, like the total number of cases or minutes allowed under this contract line.

5. Click **Save and Close**.

Tips & Tricks

➤ If your contract line allowed for 15 cases on a contract, then each time you link a case to this contract line, the number allotments will automatically reduce by 1 for each case entered into the system.

➤ The total price of the contract is calculated as the sum total price of the contract lines.

Linking service cases to a contract

It is very important to link your service cases to a service contract if you are in the kind of business where you charge for support. If your company provides free support to customers, then you can likely skip over all of the stuff in this chapter related to contracts.

Linking cases and contract lines together will ensure that your customers get their correct service allotments. It also will ensure that you don't give out any free service.

1. Open a case.

2. Locate the Contract field. Click the **lookup button** to the right of this field and choose a contract.

3. Just under the Contract field, click the lookup **button** on the Contract Line field. This will bring up a list of contract lines on the contract (chosen in step 2). Choose a contract line.

➢ The system will *only* display valid/current contracts. So, if a contract is expired or hasn't yet been invoiced, then you won't be able to link a case to it.

Invoicing a contract

Once a contract is ready to activate, you should invoice it. Only invoiced contracts will show up in the system as current contract. Anything that hasn't been invoiced is just pending.

Once a contract has been invoiced, it cannot be edited or deleted. Contracts are only valid between the start and end dates after they have been invoiced.

Step-by-Step Instructions

1. Open a contract that has at least one contract line.

2. Click **Invoice Contract** in the Actions group of the ribbon.

Tips & Tricks

➢ If you invoice a contract, it becomes read-only. There is no way to un-invoice a contract, so your only option if you need to change the terms of the contract would be to renew the contract and then delete the original contract.

Copying/renewing a contract

Have you done such a good job servicing that your customer has decided to renew his or her service contract? Give yourself a pat on the back and renew the service contract in Microsoft Dynamic CRM.

Only active/invoiced contracts can be renewed, and renewing a contract can copy over all of the information from the original contract, including contract lines.

Step-by-Step Instructions

1.   Open an active contract.

2.   Click **Renew Contract** in the Actions group of the ribbon.

3.   Select whether you'd like to include canceled contract lines.

4.   Click **OK**.

Tips & Tricks

➢   Only invoiced contracts can be renewed, but pre-invoiced contracts can be copied. Just open the contract and click Actions | Copy Contract.

➢   In the Settings | Administration | Auto-Numbering, you can modify the default format for the automatically generated contract numbers that are assigned to each contract.

18

The Articles Library

Searching or browsing knowledge base articles ◆ *Creating a new knowledge base template* ◆ *Creating a new knowledge base article from a template* ◆ *Submitting and approving knowledge base articles* ◆ *Adding comments to a knowledge base article* ◆ *Attaching an article to an outgoing e-mail*

Searching or browsing the articles library

Do you know everything? Likely not. For those times when you don't know the customer's answer off the top of your head, CRM has an articles library – a searchable database of bug fixes, how-to's, and other great document.

The articles library is a fantastic resource that allows you to manage and use all of the documents that help you resolve service cases.

Step-by-Step Instructions

1. Click **Service** on the **Navigation Pane**, and then click **Articles**.

2. Configure your search by clicking on the various buttons in the **Options** group of the Search tab on the ribbon. (For example, you might click Full-Text Search).

3. Run your search in the **Quick Find** field.

Tips & Tricks

➤ You can also browse knowledge base documents by subject. Instead of choosing the Full Text Search option, select Subject Search.

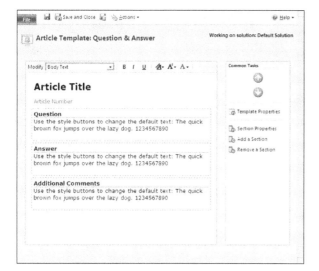

Creating an article template

Before you begin creating articles, you need to create an article template. An article template is basically a framework on which subsequent articles will be based.

The template contains the main sections that will appear in the actual documents. For example, you might create a template that includes a section to identify the question, another section to identify the answer, and a third section to identify additional resources.

1. Click **Settings** on the **Navigation Pane**, then **Business,** and then click **Templates.**

2. Click **Article Templates.**

3. Click the **New** button on the Actions toolbar.

4. Give your template a title and any sections that you want to the template.

5. Click **Save and Close.**

Tips & Tricks

➢ Basic article templates include a question section and an answer section. Add more sections to meet your business requirements.

Creating a new article from a template

You want to make life easier for your fellow service technicians, right? Then create an article after you have resolved a case.

Once the issue is in the articles library, other service technicians will be able to solve the same problem quickly and efficiently.

Step-by-Step Instructions

1. Click **Service** on the **Navigation Pane**, and then click **Articles**.

2. Click **New** button in the Records group of the ribbon.

3. Select a template and click OK.

4. Fill out the knowledge base article and click **Save and Close**.

Tips & Tricks

➤ You can only create knowledge base documents from a template. There is no freeform ability to create an article.

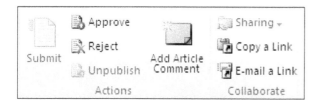

Submitting and approving articles

You'll want to be careful about what gets published in the articles library. Your fellow service technicians wouldn't like it very much if you made a mistake in one of your articles. Articles initially entered into the database show in draft form.

Once you're comfortable with an article you've written, you can submit it for approval. Articles submitted for approval can be approved, and once they're approved, they'll show up for other members of your team.

Step-by-Step Instructions

1. Click **Service** on the **Navigation Pane**, and then click **Articles**.

2. Select the **Unapproved Articles** view.

3. Highlight an article.

4. Click **Publish** in the Actions group of the ribbon.

Tips & Tricks

➢ Only certain security roles have the permission to publish articles.

Adding comments to an article

Do you have a little bit of extra information that needs to be added to the articles library, but doesn't actually need its own article? Is a particular article not up to date?

Have you found an alternate workaround for a process described in article? All of these scenarios are perfect examples of situations where your team would benefit from adding a comment to an article.

Step-by-Step Instructions

1. Open an article.

2. Click **Add Article Comment** in the Actions group of the ribbon.

3. Enter in your Comment and click OK.

Tips & Tricks

➢ If you see an error in an article, you could add a comment if you don't have security permissions to revise the article itself.

Attaching an article to an outgoing e-mail

Remember how earlier when you learned how to attach a sales literature document to an outgoing e-mail?

Fortunately, you can also attach articles to outgoing e-mails. This might be useful for a customer service caseworker who wants to e-mail an article to a contact in your database

Step-by-Step Instructions

1. Open a new e-mail in Outlook.

2. In the CRM group of the ribbon, click the **Insert Article** drop-down.

3. Select an article and click OK.

Tips & Tricks

➢ This function is only available in Outlook 2010.

19

Using Reports

Running SQL Server Reporting Services reports

So you have a bunch of data. Now you're going to need in a report form so that you can actually understand it.

SQL Server Reporting Services (SSRS) is the reporting service built right into Microsoft Dynamics CRM, so if you want to work with reports without leaving CRM, then use SSRS reports.

CRM Online gives you a wizard that makes it easy to create SSRS reports - without the need for a programmer or staff person with report writing skills.

Step-by-Step Instructions

1. Click **Workplace**, then **My Work** on the **Navigation Pane**, and then click **Reports**.

2. You can also go to a list of records and click **Reports** in the Data group of the ribbon.

Creating new reports with the report wizard

The process of creating a report is traditionally a pretty complicated process. Fortunately you can create a report by using a simple wizard in Microsoft Dynamics CRM. All you'll need to know is what you want your report to show.

Reports created with this wizard can print to your printer, can be saved as a PDF file, or they can be saved as an editable Excel spreadsheet.

Step-by-Step Instructions

1. Click **Workplace** on the **Navigation Pane**, then **My Work**, and then click **Reports**.

2. Click **New** in the Records group of the ribbon.

3. Click the **Report Wizard**.

4. Start a new report and click **Next**.

5. Follow the instructions to create the structure of your report.

Tips & Tricks

➢ Instead of using the Report Wizard to create a report, consider using Excel and Pivot Tables to accomplish the same thing. You'll find that it's a lot more flexible to do the reports in Excel.

20

Using Dashboards

Viewing your dashboards ◆ Drilling down charts on a dashboard ◆ Expanding a chart on a dashboard ◆ Viewing detailed data for a chart ◆ Creating a chart ◆ Creating a dashboard ◆ Sharing a dashboard with others

Viewing your dashboards

Admittedly, long lists of records can get a little boring. Staring at them day after day can really get to you. That's why CRM has Dashboards.

Dashboards allow you to create a visual workplace to display the data in your database. The functionality of dashboards is immense, and we'll go over some of the possibilities in the next few pages.

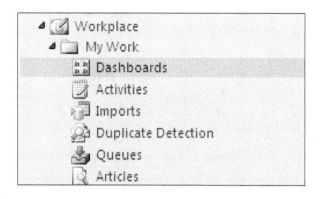

Step-by-Step Instructions

1. Click **Workplace** on the **Navigation Pane**, then **My Work**, and then click **Dashboards.**

2. You dashboards will appear. Click the drop-down above the dashboard to switch between your various dashboards

Tips & Tricks

➢ In the upper-right corner of any dashboard chart, you'll see a button that will expand the chart to full screen. There's also a button that will show a list of data used to display the chart.

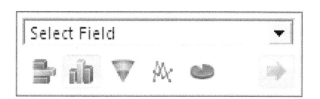

Drilling down chards on a dashboard

You're looking at the pie chart. It has a slice. The slice looks big. Impressive, even. But looks can be deceiving.

By drilling down into the data on your dashboard charts, you can see a specific list of the data represented in each slice of a pie or each bar in a bar graph.

Step-by-Step Instructions

1. Click **Workplace** on the **Navigation Pane**, then **My Work**, and then click **Dashboards**.

2. Locate a chart. Click on the data set in the chart that you want to drill down into.

3. Select a field and a chart type.

Tips & Tricks

➢ Click the X icon in the corner of the chart to return to your original chart.

Expanding a chart on a dashboard

You probably have placed multiple charts on your dashboard. This means that those charts might be small and hard to read.

This problem is easily solved by enlarging a chart on your dashboard. You can enlarge a chart and quickly return to your original dashboard by closing the chart.

Step-by-Step Instructions

1. Click **Workplace** on the **Navigation Pane**, then **My Work**, and then click **Dashboards.**

2. Locate a chart on your dashboard and click the **Enlarge your Chart** icon in the top right corner.

Tips & Tricks

➢ Consider using the built-in Snipping tool in Windows 7 to take a snapshot of this full-screen dashboard. Then, paste the dashboard into a PowerPoint presentation or Word document.

Viewing detailed data for a chart

Maybe you're crazy. Maybe you would rather look at a list of data than a nice pie chart. Then you can view the detailed data for a chart.

In all seriousness, this is a very useful function in CRM. It allows you to quickly see and analyze the source data list for a chart.

1. Click **Workplace** on the **Navigation Pane**, then **My Work**, and then click **Dashboards**.

2. Locate a chart on your dashboard and click the view source records icon in the top right corner.

➢ Click the Export to Excel button at the top of the screen to export this list of data for further analysis.

Creating a chart

Before you create a dashboard, you'll need to first create a chart. Charts in CRM display data in your system visually for you to analyze. You can create many different types of charts in CRM, including pie charts, bar graphs, and sales pipelines.

Step-by-Step Instructions

1. Go to a type of record. For example, you could click **Sales** on the **Navigation Pane**, and then click **Contacts**.

2. Click the **Charts** tab on the ribbon.

3. Click **New Chart**.

4. Give your chart a name, and specify the X and Y axis labels.

Tips & Tricks

➤ This process will create a personal chart. Personal charts are available just for you, but you can also create a system chart that will be available for all users. That's done in the Settings | Customization | Customize the System area.

Creating a dashboard

Now you're ready to create a dashboard. They may seem complicated, but CRM makes it really easy.

The create wizard does most of the work for you. The following steps describe the process involved in making a personal dashboard.

Step-by-Step Instructions

1. Click **Workplace** on the **Navigation Pane**, then **My Work**, and then click **Dashboards**.

2. Click **New** on the ribbon.

3. Select a dashboard layout and click **Next**.

4. Configure your dashboard and then click the Save & Close button when you are done.

Tips & Tricks

➤   This process creates a personal dashboard. You can also create system dashboards that are viewable for all users. That's done in the customization area. (Settings | Customization | Customize the System.)

Sharing a dashboard with others

Don't be greedy. Whenever you create a dashboard, you are assigned ownership. If you created a nice dashboard, your other co-workers can't use it until you share it with them.

You can share a dashboard with another user or team. Sharing a personal dashboard is similar to sharing a personal view.

Step-by-Step Instructions

1. Click **Workplace** in the **Navigation Pane,** then **My Work**, and then click **Dashboards**.

2. Navigate to a dashboard.

3. Click **Share Dashboard** on the ribbon.

Tips & Tricks

➢ You can share a dashboard with any user or team. If you regularly need to share dashboards with multiple users, consider creating a team of users and then share the dashboard with the team.

➢ You may also find it useful to create a team that contains all users.

21

Exporting to Excel

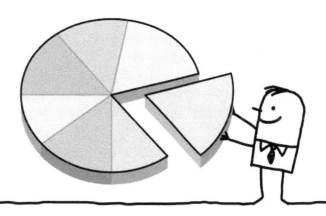

Exporting a view to Excel ◆ *Exporting an Advanced Find to Excel* ◆ *Exporting to Excel for cleanup and re-import* ◆ *Creating a pivot table in Excel 2007/2010*

Exporting a view to Excel

Many people prefer to use Microsoft Office Excel to make reports of their data. It can be a bit easier to analyze data if it is in spreadsheet form, and Excel is a very powerful tool for generating reports. It's certainly easier to learn Excel than it is to learn a complex report writer.

If you want to export a specific group of records to Excel, you can then create pivot tables, pie charts, bar graphs, or other complex analysis right within Excel.

Step-by-Step Instructions

1. Go to any list of records and select a view under the view drop-down.

2. Click the **Export to Excel** button in the Data group of the ribbon.

3. Choose to export a static worksheet and click export.

4. Click **Open**.

Tips & Tricks

➤ Exporting a dynamic spreadsheet generally won't work in CRM Online. Dynamic exports in CRM Online require that you have offline access enabled and only pull data from your local instance of SQL, not from the live server.

Export Data to Excel
Select the type of worksheet to export.

Use this type of worksheet:

● Static worksheet with records from this page

○ Dynamic PivotTable

○ Dynamic worksheet

Select Columns

Edit Columns

☑ Make this data available for re-importing by including required column headings

⚠ We recommend that you save the exported file before you open it.

Export   Cancel

Exporting an Advanced Find to Excel

Do you have a really specific set of records that needs to be exported to Excel? By running an Advanced Find and then exporting the search results to Excel, you can limit the amount of data that gets exported to Excel.

Plus, since you can change the columns that appear in your Advanced Find, you can use this method of export to get a very specific subset of your database into Excel.

Step-by-Step Instructions

1. Run an Advanced Find

2. Click **the Export to Excel** button on the toolbar.

3. Choose to export a static worksheet and click export.

4. Click **Open**.

Tips & Tricks

➤ The view that determines the default set of columns displayed when an Advanced Find is executed is called the Advanced Find view. Each entity has one, and the administrator can edit this default view in Settings | Customizations | Customize the System | Choose an entity | Forms & Views.

Exporting to Excel for cleanup and re-import

Let's be honest: you probably don't want to do any major data cleanup in CRM. After all, you can't view more that 250 records on a page at once!

It's much better to Export you data to Excel for cleanup and then re-import it once you are done.

Step-by-Step Instructions

1. Export data to Excel.

2. Clean up your data and save the spreadsheet.

3. Import the spreadsheet into CRM.

Export Data to Excel
Select the type of worksheet to export.

Use this type of worksheet:

- Static worksheet with records from this page
- Dynamic PivotTable
- Dynamic worksheet

☑ Make this data available for re-importing by including required column headings
⚠ We recommend that you save the exported file before you open it.

Export   Cancel

☑ Make this data available for re-importing by including required column headings
⚠ We recommend that you save the exported file before you open it.

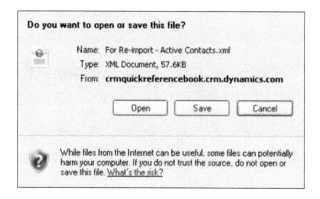

Do you want to open or save this file?

Name: For Re-import - Active Contacts.xml
Type: XML Document, 57.6KB
From: crmquickreferencebook.crm.dynamics.com

Open   Save   Cancel

While files from the Internet can be useful, some files can potentially harm your computer. If you do not trust the source, do not open or save this file. What's the risk?

Creating a pivot table in Excel 2007/2010

Pivot tables in Excel 2007 or 2007 follow the same basic concepts as pivot tables in Excel 2003, but the implementation of the feature is significantly different.

Step-by-Step Instructions

1. Export data to Excel.

2. Save the spreadsheet. You can only run pivot tables on spreadsheets that have been saved.

3. Click **Insert** on the ribbon. Click **Pivot Table** and choose the option to either create a pivot table or a pivot table with a pivot chart.

4. Configure your pivot table or pivot chart. For more information, go to bit.ly/pivot2007.

Tips & Tricks

➢ Do a Youtube or Bing search for "Pivot Tables" for some great resources and videos that will guide you through the process of creating pivot tables and pivot charts.

22

Adding and Removing Users

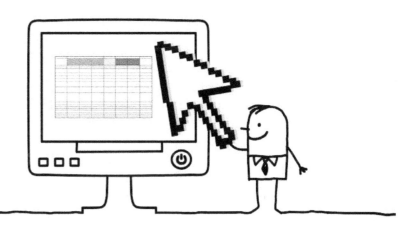

Adding a new user ◆ *Deactivating users and reassigning data* ◆ *Defining security roles* ◆ *Buying additional licenses* ◆ *Creating teams of users* ◆ *Creating business units* ◆ *Changing a user's Windows Live ID* ◆ *Resending an invitation*

Adding a new user

Do you want the co-worker in the next cubicle to experience the same euphoria you get from using Microsoft Dynamics CRM? Then add him or her as a new user.

Don't get ahead of yourself, though. If you don't have the licensing to do so, you can't add a new user.

Step-by-Step Instructions

1. Click **Settings** on the **Navigation Pane**, then **System**, and then click **Administration**.

2. Click **Users**.

3. Click the **New** button on the toolbar.

4. Select a business unit and click **Next**.

5. Choose a security role and click **Next**.

6. Enter in information about the user and click **Next**.

7. Click **Create New Users**.

Tips & Tricks

➢ If a user leaves your organization, you can disable the user. Click Settings | System | Administration | Users. Then, highlight the user and from the More Actions drop-down, choose the Disable option.

➢ Disabled users can't log in, and they don't count toward the number of available licenses you've purchased.

Users
Add new users. Edit information about users and deactivate user records. Manage the teams, roles, and licenses assigned to users.

Deactivating users and reassigning data

Has a Microsoft Dynamics CRM user left your organization? Don't let that license go to waste! Deactivating a user will free up a license and the former user will no longer have access to Microsoft Dynamics CRM.

Don't worry if that former user had some important data. You can reassign the data en masse to another user. (Or you could leave it as-is.)

Step-by-Step Instructions

1. Click **Settings** on the **Navigation Pane**, then **System,** and then click **Administration**.

2. Click **Users**.

3. Highlight the user that you'd like to deactivate.

4. Click the **More actions** button on the toolbar, then **Disable**.

5. Click **OK**.

6. Double-click the user record.

7. Click the Actions button on the toolbar, then Reassign Records.

8. Click **OK**.

Tips & Tricks

➢ In the list of users, go to the Disabled Users view to see users who have been disabled.

Defining user security roles

Everyone in your organization shouldn't be able to have the same security role. That's why it's important to set security roles for users in your database. Security roles define the level of access that a user has to the types of data and certain features in the data.

You might, for example, want to restrict some of your users' ability to delete certain types of records. This way, a user won't accidentally (or otherwise) delete all of the contacts in your database.

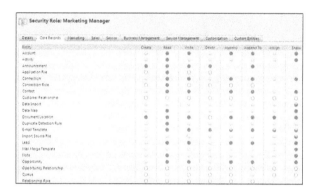

Step-by-Step Instructions

1. Click **Settings** on the **Navigation Pane**, then System, and then click **Administration**.

2. Click **Security Roles**.

3. Click the **New** button on the toolbar.

4. Give the user a name.

5. Under each tab, designate the user's level of access.

6. Click **Save and Close**.

Tips & Tricks

➤ Don't start from scratch. Take a security role that is similar to the one you're creating. Highlight that role and choose Copy Role from the More Actions drop-down.

Subscription Management
View the details of your Microsoft Dynamics CRM Online subscription, purchase additional user licenses, and manage storage.

Resource Usage and Management

User Licenses:

Purchased:	5
In Use:	3
Available:	2

To remove user licenses, call 1-877-CRM-CHOICE (1-877-276-2464)

Storage: [_____] 0.00% used (0.00 of 5.00 GB)   [Add Storage] [Remove Storage]

Review Current Charges and Select Number of Licenses

After reviewing your current charges, enter the number of user licenses you would like to purchase in the Quantity field. These licenses will be added to your Microsoft Dynamics CRM Online organization and your monthly bill will be updated to reflect the changes.

Current Monthly Charges

Unit Price	Description	Quantity	Total
$19.00	User Licenses
User licenses determine how many people you can invite to your Microsoft Dynamics CRM Online organization.	5	$95.00
$0.99
$0.0	Additional Storage
Microsoft Dynamics CRM Online includes an initial 5.0GB of storage.	0 GB	$0.00
	Total current monthly charges:		**$95.00**

How many licenses would you like to add?

Unit Price	Description	Quantity	Total
$19.00	User Licenses
(You have 5 licenses: 3 used, 2 available)	[____]	$0.00

Note: Prices do not include applicable taxes.   Updated total monthly charges: **$95.00**

Additional Storage Fee Waiver* Microsoft is waiving the $9.99 fee per GB for additional storage for the term of your subscription. The promotion is available to qualifying customers with active subscriptions in countries where Microsoft Dynamics CRM Online is available. Monthly billing of $9.99 per GB for additional storage will resume when subscription is renewed, unless otherwise notified.

[_____] [_____] [Cancel]

Buying additional licenses

Have you used up all of your licenses? Fear not! You can buy as many additional licenses as your budget (or credit card limit) will allow.

When you add an additional license, you won't be able to remove this license during the term of your contract without paying a penalty, so you wouldn't want to add licenses that you're not planning on using in the short term.

Step-by-Step Instructions

1. Click **Settings** on the **Navigation Pane**, then **System,** and then click **Administration.**

2. Click **Subscription Management.**

3. Click **Add Licenses.**

Tips & Tricks

➢ When buying more licenses, you will be able to see your new monthly total.

➢ You can also add more available storage space in the Subscription Management section.

➢ Only the billing administrator will be able to perform this task. This is generally the person who originally set up the CRM Online subscription.

Creating teams of users

You shouldn't try to take on everything yourself. Creating a team of users will help people in your organization work more efficiently with each other

Team structures in CRM are mostly used for sharing records on a one-off basis. (You'll use business units for most of your default record sharing settings. You can share any record (or a set of records) with an individual user or a team of users.

Teams
Add new teams and new members to existing teams. Modify the team description and delete members from teams.

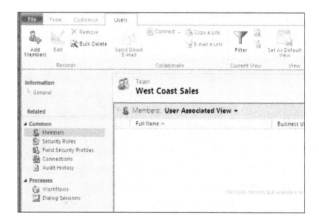

Step-by-Step Instructions

1. Click **Settings** on the **Navigation Pane**, then **System**, and then click **Administration**.

2. Click **Teams**.

3. Click the **New** button on the toolbar.

4. Give a name and business unit to your team.

5. Click **Save**. Go to the next page to add users.

Tips & Tricks

➤ To remove a user from a team, just open the user record and click the Teams option on the left.

Business Units
Add new business units. Edit and deactivate existing business units. Change the parent business unit.

Creating business units

Microsoft Dynamics CRM allows you to organize your company under different business units. You might set up business units for each individual operating unit within your company, but even if your company is small, you might also set up business units for each team or functional role within the business.

When you are creating a security role, which will determine what level of access each user has to parts of the database, one of the things you'll be able to do is restrict access to just records owned within your business unit. So, if you're in the East Coast business unit, you might only see records owned by other people in the East Coast business unit.

Step-by-Step Instructions

1. Click **Settings** on the **Navigation Pane**, then **System**, and then click **Administration**.

2. Click **Business Units**.

3. Click the **New** button on the toolbar.

4. Give the business unit a name.

5. Click **Save and Close**.

Tips & Tricks

➢ Users must belong to one (and only one) business unit.

➢ Business units cannot be deleted.

Changing a user's Windows Live ID

The Windows Live ID is the primary login mechanism for CRM Online, and you can get one for free. When you set up a user, the system will assume that this user's Windows Live ID is the same as the e-mail address that you specified when you configured the user's account.

Sometimes, though, you may need to change the Windows Live ID for a user. For example, if your organization changes domain names and your users change e-mail addresses, you'd have to change both the e-mail address *and* the Windows Live ID for your users.

Step-by-Step Instructions

1. Click **Settings** on the **Navigation Pane**, then **System**, and then click **Administration**.

2. Click **Users**.

3. Double-click a user record.

4. Click **Change Windows Live ID** in the Actions group of the ribbon.

Tips & Tricks

➢ If your users are also Hotmail users, you might want to change their WLID's to their Hotmail address. This will reduce the number of sign in/sign out frustrations they experience.

Resending an invitation

When you add a new user, you have to send an invitation to this user before he/she can login. The invitation comes in the form of an e-mail to the user.

Invitations are only valid for three days, so sometimes they need to be resent. If you set up a user recently, and the user isn't able to log in, it's likely that you will need to resend the invitation.

Step-by-Step Instructions

1. Click **Settings** on the **Navigation Pane**, then **System**, and then click **Administration**.

2. Click **Users**.

3. Double-click a user record.

4. Click **Resend Invitation** in the Actions group of the ribbon.

Tips & Tricks

➢ If the invitation emails are getting caught in your spam filters, send the invitation again and just try logging into the database (in Internet Explorer) as the user. You'll be prompted to accept the terms of use, and the system should grant your new user access to the database from that point forward.

23

Using Processes

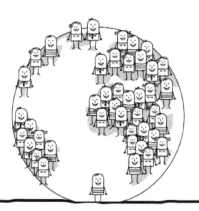

Creating a new Workflow

Workflows are like macros on steroids. A workflow can perform automated tasks, either on-demand or because some condition has been met within the database.

So, when a new opportunity is entered into the system, workflow could see that a new record has been created, and it might invoke and automatically create a follow-up task in a week and send an e-mail back to the customer thanking him/her for the opportunity to do business.

Step-by-Step Instructions

1. Click **Settings** on the **Navigation Pane**, then **Process Center,** and then click **Processes.**

2. Click **New** on the toolbar.

3. Give your workflow a name and choose the type of entity that the workflow will work with. Select Workflow as your Category.

4. Click **OK**. The workflow will appear and will be ready to add steps.

Tips & Tricks

➤ When creating a workflow, you need to specify whether the workflow will run just for yourself, for your business unit, or for the entire organization.

➤ You'll also need to specify whether the workflow will engage on-demand or when an action occurs in the database.

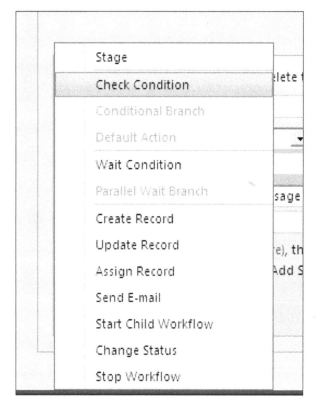

Adding Workflow steps

A workflow can be made of multiple steps. The steps could wait for something to happen, they could check for a condition within the database. Workflow can also create new records, like contacts or tasks in Outlook.

One of the workflow steps can even kill the workflow. The sum total of all of the steps in your workflow is the task that will be performed when the workflow is invoked.

1. Open an unpublished workflow.

2. In the steps area of the workflow, click the Add Step button. Choose the type of step you'd like to add.

3. Depending on the type of step you're adding, you'll have to clarify details for the step. You can add as many steps as you require. Workflow will perform each step in order.

➤ You cannot update a picklist field through workflow.

➤ Types of steps available in Workflow are: Check Condition, Wait Condition, Create Record, Update Record, Assign Record, Send E-mail, Start Child Workflow, Change Status, and End Workflow.

Activating a Workflow

When you create a workflow, the workflow is saved in a draft mode. It won't actually become available until you publish it.

This gives you a chance to work on the details of the workflow before you deploy it to the entire database. You'll want to have the option to keep a workflow in a draft form, since workflows can perform tasks that modify (and possibly destroy) the data in your system.

Step-by-Step Instructions

1. Click **Settings** on the **Navigation Pane**, then **Process Center**, and then click **Processes**.

2. Highlight the workflow you'd like to publish.

3. Click **Publish**.

Tips & Tricks

➢ You can only publish workflows that you own.

➢ Click the **Assign** button to assign a workflow to yourself if you don't have access to edit or publish a specific workflow.

Process Activate Confirmation
You have selected 1 Process to activate.

This action will attempt to activate the Process you have selected.

OK   Cancel

Workflow example: creating a follow-up task for new opportunities

In this example, we'll walk through the steps required to set Microsoft Dynamics CRM to automatically create a follow-up task whenever an opportunity is entered into the system.

1. Create a new workflow on the opportunity entity.

2. In the Options for Automatic Workflows area, choose Organization for the scope. The workflow will engage for all users.

3. In the Start When area, the only thing that should be checked is the Record is created option. This way, the workflow will only engage when a new opportunity is created.

4. Click the **Add Step** button on the toolbar and choose Create Record.

5. In the Create field, choose **Task**.

6. Click the **Set Properties** and configure how you'd like this automatic task to look in Outlook.

7. Click **Save and then Publish.**

Creating a Dialog

Dialogs are windows that pop up prompting you for certain information. You might not have ever heard of them, but you've surely run across them.

Dialogs boxes are useful for getting information cleanly into your system, especially if you have employees that aren't very enthusiastic about completing record forms.

Step-by-Step Instructions

1. Click **Settings** on the **Navigation Pane**, then **Process Center,** and then click **Processes**.

2. Click **New** on the toolbar.

3. Give your dialog a name and choose the type of entity that the dialog will work with. Select Dialog as your Category.

4. Click **OK**. The dialog will appear and will be ready to add steps.

Stage

Page

Prompt and Response

Check Condition

Conditional Branch

Default Action

Query CRM Data

Assign Value

Create Record

Update Record

Assign Record

Send E-mail

Start Child Workflow

Link Child Dialog

Change Status

Stop Dialog

24

Customizing the System

Adding new fields ◆ Setting field level security ◆ Creating global option sets (drop-down) ◆ Adding a sub-grid ◆ Modifying the default views ◆ Modifying the forms ◆ Modifying the head/footer of a form ◆ Modifying the Navigation Pane ◆ Creating a system view (save as function) ◆ Creating custom entities ◆ Publishing customizations ◆ Enabling auditing

Adding new fields

Don't like the way Microsoft Dynamics looks "out-of-the-box?" Do you want different fields to show up in a record view? Buying Microsoft Dynamics CRM is kind of like buying a house. It's a great framework, but it doesn't become a home until you configure the furniture.

Fortunately, you can easily add new fields to any record view. Customization in Microsoft Dynamics CRM is easy, and in no time you'll have the database looking the way you want it to.

Step-by-Step Instructions

1. Click **Settings** on the **Navigation Pane**, then **Customization,** and then click **Customizations**.

2. Click **Customize the System**, and then Entities.

3. Double-click an entity.

4. Click **Forms** on the left, and then double-click **Form**.

5. Click **Add Fields** under Common Tasks to add a field.

6. Select the field you want to add, then designate a tab and a section. Click OK.

7. Click **Save and Close**. Remember to publish your customizations.

Tips & Tricks

➢ Click the **Save and New** button instead of Save and Close if you are adding multiple fields.

Setting field level security

You can really make the data in your system ultra secure by setting field level security in CRM. By setting field level security, you can determine what fields users can read/edit when the open up a record form.

Step-by-Step Instructions

1. Click **Settings** on the **Navigation Pane**, then **Customization**, and then click **Customizations**.

2. Click **Customize Entities**.

3. Double-click an entity.

4. Click **Fields** on the left, then double-click a field.

5. Select the option to enable field level security.

Creating global option sets (drop-down)

Do you find yourself creating the same drop-down field over and over again on different entities? Stop right there! If you create a global option set – which is a fancy phrase fro drop down – you will only need to create it once. It can then be applied to any record form in the CRM system.

Step-by-Step Instructions

1. Click **Settings** on the **Navigation Pane**, then **Customization,** and then click **Customizations.**

2. Click **Customize the System**, and then **Option Sets.**

3. Click the **New** button.

4. Configure your new global option set.

Adding a sub-grid

A sub-grid is basically a table that displays a list of records within a record form. So, if you want to display a list of activities within the contact form, you can add a sub-grid to display these activities.

Step-by-Step Instructions

1. Click **Settings** on **the Navigation Pane,** then **Customization,** and then click **Customizations.**

2. Click **Customize the System,** and then **Entities.**

3. Double-click an entity.

4. Click **Forms** on the left, and then double-click **Form.**

5. Click **Sub-grid** on the Insert tab of the ribbon.

Tips & Tricks

➢   If you add a subgrid, consider removing the data item from the left Navigation Pane.

Modifying the default views

Whenever you look at a list of records, you're looking at a view. Go to the contacts screen in CRM, and in the upper right corner of the list of records, check out the View drop-down. This drop-down will show you the current view of records.

You might not like the way a certain view looks. You might, for example, want to add or remove the columns that show up in your Active Contacts view. Modifying the default views is easy and similar to any other entity customization that you might do in Microsoft Dynamics CRM.

Step-by-Step Instructions

1. Click **Settings** on the **Navigation Pane**, then **Customization**, and then click **Customizations**.

2. Click **Customize the System**, and then **Entities**.

3. Double-click an entity.

4. Click **Views** on the left, then highlight a view, such as Active Accounts.

5. On the More Actions drop-down, click **Set Default**.

Modifying the forms

When you open a record in Microsoft Dynamics CRM, the screen that lets you edit the record is called the form.

Forms in Microsoft Dynamics CRM are highly customizable. You can add fields, tabs, and sections to your record view. You can also move things around so everything looks the way you want it to.

Step-by-Step Instructions

1. Click **Settings** on the **Navigation Pane**, then **Customization**, and then click **Customizations**.

2. Click **Customize the System**, and then **Entities**.

3. Double-click an entity.

4. Click **Forms** on the left, and then double-click **Form**.

Tips & Tricks

➢ Click the Form Properties option to add custom javascript code to your forms.

➢ There is one form for all users. Changes made to the form will appear on everyone's system.

Modifying the header/footer of a form

Headers and footers appear at the top and bottom of each form in CRM. You have the option to hide them. But you can also edit them.   Follow the steps below to modify the header/footer on a form.

1.   Click **Settings** on the **Navigation Pane**, then **Customization**, and then click **Customization**.

2.   Click **Customize Entities.**

3.   Double-click an entity.

4.   Click **Forms** on the left.

5.   Click on the header/footer to edit them.

➢   Some fields commonly added to the header/footer are fields like name, owner, and entity-specific important fields. For example, on an opportunity record, the estimated close date might be important enough to add to the header.

Modifying the Navigation Pane

So you've customized your contact form and everything looks good except for one thing: you don't use half the options on that left Navigation Pane.

In CRM, these options can be removed from the form. So if your organization doesn't use CRM for invoices, the remove the Invoices option from the Navigation Pane.

Step-by-Step Instructions

1. Click **Settings** on the **Navigation Pane**, then **Customization,** and then click **Customizations**.

2. Click **Customize Entities.**

3. Double-click an entity.

4. Click **Forms** on the left, and then open the main form.

5. Double-click the **Navigation Pane.** You can now drag and remove items on the pane.

Tips & Tricks

➢ Don't forget to double-click in the Navigation Pane. That's the only way you'll be able to remove items from it.

Creating a system view

Earlier in this book we covered creating a personal view. Only a user can view a personal view, unless it is shared? How, then, do you make views that are available to the entire organization?

System views are views that are available to all of the users in your database. Follow the steps below to create a system view.

Step-by-Step Instructions

1. Click **Settings** on the **Navigation Pane**, then **Customization**, and then click **Customizations**.

2. Click **Customize Entities.**

3. Select an entity on the left click Views.

4. Click **Views** on the left.

5. Open a view. Make any changes and click the **Save As** button.

Tips & Tricks

➢ You can also create a system view from scratch.

Creating custom entities

Types of records in Microsoft Dynamics CRM are called entities. Contacts, accounts, tasks, sales literature, and opportunities are all examples of entities that exist with an out-of-the-box CRM database.

Your organization might want to keep track of an entity that doesn't with Microsoft Dynamics CRM. Don't worry, though, because it's really easy to create custom entities in Microsoft Dynamics CRM.

Step-by-Step Instructions

1. Click **Settings** on the **Navigation Pane**, then **Customization**, and then click **Customizations**.

2. Click **Customize the System.** Then, on the left, click **Entities**.

3. Click New.

4. Enter in information about your entity and click **Save and Close.**

Tips & Tricks

➢ You can also change the name of any existing entity. For example, you might change Accounts to Companies. In the list of entities, just double-click an entity and you'll have the option to change its name.

Publishing customizations

Hold it right there. Just because you've done a customization doesn't mean that it will show up in your database.

No changes that you make to the database will show up until you publish your customizations.

Step-by-Step Instructions

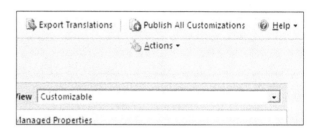

1. Click **Settings** on the **Navigation Pane**, then **Customization**, and then click **Customizations**.

2. Click **Customize the System**.

3. Click **Publish All Customizations**.

Tips & Tricks

➤ You can export a backup of your customizations at any time. Click Settings | Customization | Customizations | Solutions.

➤ You can then import customizations by clicking Settings | Customizations | Solutions.

Enabling auditing

You're going to want to know what's going on in your database. You don't, for example, want your salespeople to be fudging their sales figures. This is why you should consider enabling auditing in your system.

Step-by-Step Instructions

1. Click **Settings** on the **Navigation Pane**, then **System**, and then click **Auditing**.

2. Click **Global Audit Settings**.

3. Configure your **Audit Settings**.

Tips & Tricks

➢ Be careful about auditing every record in your system. This will overload your system with data that you never use.

Enabling auditing for an entity/field

Having an audit record of absolutely everything in your database might be unreasonable. It would take up way too much space.

Instead, you should define which entities/fields in your system should be audited. This way you can keep track of the important changes in your database, and still not be overburdened with audit data.

1. Click **Settings** on the **Navigation Pane**, then **Customization**, and then click **Customizations**.

2. Click **Customize the System**.

3. Expand **Entities**, then expand a **specific entity**, and then **Fields**. Double-click **a field**.

4. Change the **Auditing** field to **Enable**.

5. Click **Save and Close**.

➢ You need to complete the steps on the previous page to enable auditing for an entity/field.

Viewing the Audit Summary view

Once you've configured auditing in your system, you'll want to view the audit summary. This is a view where you can look at all of the changes made to entities/records in your database.

1. Click **Settings** on the **Navigation Pane**, then **System**, and then click **Auditing**.

2. Click **Audit Summary** view.

➤ You could export the Audit Summary view to Excel for further analysis. PivotTables in Excel are especially useful for analyzing audit logs.

➤ The Audit Summary view is also a great place to see who is using your system, how often they are making changes, and (perhaps most importantly) who isn't using CRM.

25

Administrative Functions

Installing the Outlook plugin ◆ *Updating the plugin to the latest build* ◆ *Setting the default number of records that show per page* ◆ *Turning off the e-mail tracking token* ◆ *Auto-creating records for tracked e-mails* ◆ *Setting your default view for a list* ◆ *Turning off the Getting Started Panes* ◆ *Specifying contacts that should sync down to Outlook* ◆ *Forcing a synchronization* ◆ *Working offline* ◆ *Linknig CRM with SharePoint*

Installing the Outlook plug-in

You always have Outlook open. If you don't, you're probably not working anyway. One of the greatest features of Microsoft Dynamics CRM is that you can access all of your data directly within Outlook. There isn't another button to click. There aren't other windows to open. If you have e-mail up, you also have your database open.

If you are familiar with Outlook, then getting used to Microsoft Dynamics CRM for Outlook should be a cinch.

Step-by-Step Instructions

1. On a computer that doesn't have the Outlook plug-in installed, log into your Microsoft Dynamics CRM database by going to **yoursite.crm.dynamics.com** in Internet Explorer.

2. Click the CRM for Outlook button on the toolbar.

3. Run the client installer when prompted.

Tips & Tricks

➤   If in doubt, choose the option to install *without* offline access. Installing the Outlook plug-in will install a local instance of MS SQL

Welcome
to Microsoft Update

Checking for the latest updates for your computer...

Updating the plug-in to the latest build

Did your computer freeze? Before you swear off technology completely, update Microsoft Dynamics CRM to the latest build. This will make sure that you have the latest version of the product with the newest bug-fixes and features.

The CRM plug-in updates are automatically bundled in with Windows Updates. So updating the CRM plug-in is as simple as performing a Windows update.

Step-by-Step Instructions

1.   In Internet Explorer, go to **www.microsoftupdate.com.**

2.   Updates to CRM are delivered through Microsoft update. Follow the instructions on the screen to set Microsoft Update to automatically download updates for CRM.

Tips & Tricks

➢   You'll need to be connected to the Internet to perform an update.

➢   If you already have the latest build of the software, the update will let you know that everything is up-to-date.

Setting the default startup screen

If you are a service technician, you probably want the Cases screen to pop up when you first open Microsoft Dynamics CRM. If you are a salesperson, it might be useful to have the system automatically open to your list of open opportunities.

You can change the default startup screen in Microsoft Dynamics CRM. Both the default pane and tab can be set.

Step-by-Step Instructions

1. Click the **File** tab on the menu.

2. Click **Options**.

3. Select the default pane and tab.

Tips & Tricks

➢ Each user has his/her own default startup screen.

➢ This applies to CRM users who use Internet Explorer to log in.
Outlook users can ignore this page.

Setting the default number of records show per page

Is that big list of records a bit overwhelming? Or are you a data fiend who wants even more records to show up on one page? Either way, you're in luck.

Microsoft Dynamics CRM lets you set the default number of records that show up on a page. The default is 50, but most users find it more useful to show 250 records per page.

Step-by-Step Instructions

1. Click the **File** tab on the ribbon

2. Click **Options**.

3. Under the **General** tab, set the default number of records.

Tips & Tricks

➢ There is no way to view more than 250 records per page on any CRM entity.

➢ If you need to see more than 250 records at a time, export to Excel and analyze your data in Excel.

Turning off the e-mail tracking token

If you've sent e-mail that is tracked in the CRM database, you've probably noticed that CRM appends a long string of numbers to the end of outgoing e-mail messages.

This string of text is called the tracking token and looks something like this: CRM:001002034. If a customer responds to this e-mail and leaves the tracking token intact, then the response from the customer is also tracked in CRM.

Many customers don't like the looks of the tracking token, and turning it off only removes the automatic tracking of responses.

Step-by-Step Instructions

1. Click **Settings** on the **Navigation Pane**, then **System**, and then click **Administration**.

2. Click **System Settings**.

3. Click the **E-mail** tab.

4. Uncheck the **Use Tracking Token** option.

Tips & Tricks

➢ If you decide to use the e-mail tracking token, you can change the format of the token by clicking Settings | Administration | Auto-Numbering.

Auto-creating records for tracked e-mails

The less time you spend in CRM performing menial tasks the better. That's why you should learn how to set up CRM so that it automatically creates records for tracked e-mails.

This way, if you track an e-mail in CRM, you can automatically create a contact record for that e-mail, provided there is no matching contact already in the system.

Step-by-Step Instructions

1. Click on the **File** tab and then CRM. (Or just click on the File tab if you are accessing from Internet Explorer.)

2. Click **Options**.

3. Click the **E-mail** tab.

4. Check the option to create records for tracked e-mails.

Tips & Tricks

➢ This feature is only available if you have the Outlook plugin installed.

Setting your default view for a list

Do you find yourself primarily using one view of a certain entity in CRM? But whenever you click on an entity in the Navigation Pane, CRM opens a view that you never use?

To solve this issue, you can set your default view for a list. A default view will then automatically be the first view that pops up when you click on an entity, such as contacts.

Step-by-Step Instructions

1. Click on an entity in the **Navigation Pane**, such as **Contacts**.

2. On the View tab, click **Set as Default View**.

Tips & Tricks

➢ You don't have the option to set a default view in CRM for Outlook. Instead, you pin a view.

Turning off the Getting Started Panes

So you've gotten to the point where you know your way around CRM pretty well. But those Getting Started panes, that were so useful when you first began using CRM, are now getting in your way.

Follow the directions below to remove the Getting Started Panes from CRM.

Step-by-Step Instructions

1. Click **Settings** on the **Navigation Pane**, then **System**, and then click **Administration**.

2. Click **System Settings**.

3. Click the E-**mail** tab.

4. Choose the option to not show the Getting Started Panes.

Tips & Tricks

➢ By following these steps you will remove the Getting Started Panes for everyone in your database. Individual users can also remove them under Personal Options.

Specifying contacts that should sync down to Outlook

CRM won't sync to your phone, but Outlook does, so any CRM contacts you sync down to Outlook will likely instantly show up on your phone.

Changes made to the contact record on your phone will sync back into Outlook. Then, they'll sync from Outlook back into CRM. All of this happens over-the-air.

Step-by-Step Instructions

1. In Outlook, click the **File** tab, then **CRM**, and then **Options**.

2. On the **Synchronization** tab, click the **Outlook Filters** option.

3. Double click **My Outlook Contacts.** The query that appears represents the set of contacts that will sync from CRM down into Outlook.

Tips & Tricks

➢ For help on building queries, take a look at the Advanced Find lessons in this book.

➢ Contacts currently in Outlook will not sync up to CRM, unless you click the Track button.

➢ Sync happens every 15 minutes. To run a manual sync, click CRM on the menu and choose Synchronize with CRM.

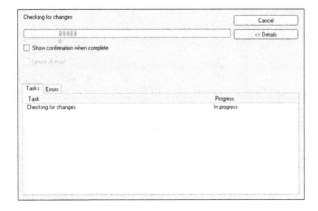

Forcing a synchronization

Microsoft Dynamics CRM for Outlook synchronizes contacts, appointments, and tasks automatically every fifteen minutes. But if you are really impatient, you can force synchronization.

You'll only really need to use this if you need to see changes synchronized right away. For example, if you've updated an appointment in CRM and your boss is yelling because he can't see it in Outlook, you'd need to force a sync (or wait for fifteen minutes).

Step-by-Step Instructions

1.   Click **File** on the the **CRM** tab.

2.   Click **Synchronize with CRM** in the Actions group of the ribbon.

Tips & Tricks

➤   Your administrator can set the default sync increment for Outlook. 15 minutes is as often as it can happen, though.

➤   Normally, you won't have to force a sync. Only run these steps when you suspect something isn't synchronizing properly or if you need to see something passed from CRM <-> Outlook instantly.

Working offline

Have you decided to spend some time in a cave with no electricity or internet? Well, the offline access feature is just for you! Working offline allows you to disconnect from the Microsoft Dynamics CRM server and still work with records in your database.

When you go offline, Microsoft Dynamics CRM synchronizes selected parts of your CRM database to your local computer. Your changes will synchronize with the online database once you re-enter civilization and connect to the Internet.

Step-by-Step Instructions

1. Click the **CRM** tab.

2. Click **Go Offline** in the Actions group of the ribbon.

Tips & Tricks

➤ Avoid working offline. It increases the need your need to troubleshoot. It would be better to get a wireless internet card.

Document Management Settings   ⦿ Help

Select entities
Document management will be enabled on the selected entities.

	Entities
☐	Entities
☑	Account
☐	Address
☐	Appointment
☑	Article
☐	Business Unit
☐	Campaign
☐	Campaign Activity
☐	Campaign Response
☐	Case
☐	Case Resolution
☐	Competitor

Set automatic folder creation settings
Folders will be automatically created if the site is a SharePoint Server 2010 site and has the List component installed on it.

URL: Specify SharePoint 2010 Site URL

[Next]   [Cancel]

Linking CRM with SharePoint

Earlier in this book we covered attaching SharePoint articles to a record. There are many possibilities when you integrate SharePoint with CRM. But before you can do any of this, you will need to link SharePoint with CRM.

Step-by-Step Instructions

1. Click **Settings** on the Navigation Pane, then **System**, and then click **Document Management**.

2. Enter your **SharePoint URL** and make sure there is a checkmark next to every entity where you would like to use SharePoint for document management.

3. Click Next, and follow the instructions to set additional SharePoint options.

Tips & Tricks

➢ Obviously, you will need to have a SharePoint server in place before you can integrate CRM and SharePoint.

Appendix

System Requirements & Recommendations

Minimum Hardware Requirements

The table below shows the absolute minimum requirements for using CRM Online with the Outlook plugin installed. It's important to note that this list shows the requirements, not the recommendations. If you have the hardware on this list, then CRM will open. It may be painfully slow, but it will open. Go to the Recommendations section to see the kind of hardware that you should realistically have.

Source: Microsoft Dynamics CRM Implementation Guide

Component	Minimum Hardware
Processor (32-bit)	750-MHz CPU, or comparable
Processor (64-bit)	x64 architecture or compatible 1.5 GHz processor
Memory	2-GB RAM
Hard disk	1.5 GB of available hard disk space
Display	Super VGA with a resolution of 1024 x 768

* Actual requirements and product functionality may vary based on your system configuration and operating system.

Successful network installation of Microsoft Dynamics CRM for Outlook requires a reliable and high-throughput network. Otherwise, installation might fail. The recommended minimum available bandwidth of the network connection is 300 Kbps.

Hardware Recommendations

This table lists the hardware that you should have in-place to run Microsoft Dynamics CRM with the Outlook plug-in. You can still use CRM if you have hardware older than this, but your experience may be sluggish.

Source: *Microsoft Dynamics CRM Implementation Guide*

Component	*Recommended Hardware
Processor (32-bit)	Multi-core 1.8-GHz CPU or higher
Processor (64-bit)	Multi-core x64 architecture 2GHz CPU or higher such as AMD Opteron or Intel Xeon systems
Memory	4-GB RAM or more
Hard disk	2 GB of available hard disk space
Display	Super VGA with a resolution higher than 1024 x 768

Outlook Plug-in Software Recommendations

The following software must be in place if you are planning on using Microsoft Dynamics CRM with the Outlook plug-in.

Source: *Microsoft Dynamics CRM Implementation Guide*

- **Microsoft Internet Explorer**

    - Internet Explorer 7 or a later version
    - Internet Explorer 8 or a later version
    - Microsoft Internet Explorer 6 or earlier versions are **not** supported.

- **Microsoft Office**

    - Microsoft Office 2003 with SP3 or later version
    - 2007 Microsoft Office system
    - Office 2010
    - Indexing Service (must be installed and running)
    - Microsoft Office XP and Microsoft Outlook 2000 versions are **not** supported for installing and running Microsoft Dynamics CRM for Outlook.
    - To install and run the 64-bit version of Microsoft Dynamics CRM for Outlook, a 64-bit version of Office 2010 is required.

- **Outlook Profile**

    - Before you run the Configuration Wizard to configure Microsoft Dynamics CRM for Outlook, a Microsoft Office Outlook profile must exist for the user. Therefore, Outlook must be run at least once to create the user's Outlook profile.

- **Installed During Setup**
  The following programs are not required prior to installation of the Outlook plug-in, but they will be installed during the plug-in setup.

    - Microsoft SQL Server 2008 Express Edition (Microsoft Dynamics CRM for Outlook with Offline Access only)
    - Microsoft .NET Framework 4.0
    - Microsoft Windows Installer (MSI) 4.5.
    - MSXML 4.0
    - Microsoft Visual C++ Redistributable
    - Microsoft Report Viewer 2010
    - Microsoft Application Error Reporting

- Windows Identity Framework (WIF)

- **Operating Systems**
  Any one of the following operating systems is required:

  - Windows 7 (both 64-bit and 32-bit versions)
  - Windows Vista (both 64-bit and 32-bit versions)
  - Microsoft Windows XP Professional SP3
  - Microsoft Windows XP Tablet SP3
  - Windows XP Professional x64 Edition
  - **Important:** Windows XP Media Center Edition is **not** supported for installing and running Microsoft Dynamics CRM for Outlook.

Web Client Software Recommendations

The following software must be in place if you are planning on using Microsoft Dynamics CRM in Internet Explorer.

Source: Microsoft Dynamics CRM Implementation Guide

- ***Operating System***

  - Windows 7 (all versions)
  - Windows Vista (all versions)
  - Microsoft Windows XP Professional SP3
  - Microsoft Windows XP Home SP3
  - Windows XP Media Center Edition SP3
  - Microsoft Windows XP Tablet SP3

- **Internet Explorer**

  - Internet Explorer 8 or a later version
  - Internet Explorer 7 or a later version

- **Office Integration**

  - Microsoft Office 2003 SP3 or later version
  - 2007 Microsoft Office system SP2 or later version
  - Office 2010
  - Note: Microsoft Windows 2000 editions are **not** supported for installing and running the Microsoft Dynamics CRM Web client.

Index

Microsoft Dynamics CRM Online Quick Reference

Index

www.ingramcontent.com/pod-product-compliance
Lightning Source LLC
Chambersburg PA
CBHW080401060326

40689CB00019B/4094